Becoming an Industrial-Organizational Psychologist

So you want to be an Industrial-Organizational (I-O) Psychologist? You may have heard that it is one of the fields of the future, fast-growing, and a highly sought-after profession. But what is Industrial-Organizational Psychology? What does an Industrial-Organizational Psychologist do? Answering these questions and many more, *Becoming an Industrial-Organizational Psychologist* is the perfect introduction, providing an expert overview of careers in Industrial-Organizational Psychology, the study of human behavior in the workplace.

Part 1 of the book discusses what I-O Psychology is and what I-O Psychologists do, including the history of the field, research areas, and job types and titles. Part 2 discusses the undergraduate years, including how to make oneself competitive for graduate school, and going through the process of identifying graduate programs, applying, and deciding on the right program. Part 3 focuses on the graduate years, including advice on success in a graduate program and in internships, as well as additional issues like licensure and transitioning from other careers. Finally, Part 4 discusses how to find a job and begin a career in the various sectors of I-O Psychology: academic, consulting, industry, and government.

Dennis Doverspike is the President of Doverspike Consulting, LLC. He recently retired from his position as Full Professor of Psychology at The University of Akron, and has authored three books and over 200 other publications in Industrial-Organizational Psychology.

Catalina Flores is a Ph.D. Candidate in Industrial-Organizational Psychology at The University of Akron.

Becoming an Industrial-Organizational Psychologist

*Dennis Doverspike and
Catalina Flores*

Routledge
Taylor & Francis Group

NEW YORK AND LONDON

First published 2019
by Routledge
52 Vanderbilt Avenue, New York, NY 10017

and by Routledge
2 Park Square, Milton Park, Abingdon, Oxon, OX14 4RN

Routledge is an imprint of the Taylor & Francis Group, an informa business

© 2019 Taylor & Francis

Library of Congress Cataloging-in-Publication Data
A catalog record for this title has been requested

ISBN: 978-1-138-48068-1 (hbk)
ISBN: 978-1-138-48069-8 (pbk)
ISBN: 978-1-351-06186-5 (ebk)

Typeset in Bembo
by Swales & Willis Ltd

For Dennis Doverspike

To my golfing buddy, Dan Campbell, who passed away as we were submitting the book to the publisher. His friendship will be greatly missed.

For Catalina Flores

To Alma, Victor, and Nora, mis tesoros.

Contents

Tables

Textboxes

Preface

OUR STORIES

I understand you are curious about becoming an Industrial-Organizational Psychologist (usually abbreviated to an I-O Psychologist), which explains why you have picked up this book. Yes, I, Dennis Doverspike, admit that I am an I-O Psychologist. It is my pleasure to be able to share my perspective of as both an I-O practitioner and a professor in one of the top I-O programs in the United States. For better or for worse, I have many years of experience; yes, at this point I have even engaged in the final career stage of retirement, a phasedown leading to full-time retirement, at least as an academic.

Given I have become something of an elder statesman, I find that my stories and anecdotes are often lost on my students. When I refer to a classic television show such as *Seinfeld*, my students get this blank look and relate that not only have they never seen *Seinfeld*, they also do not own a television, preferring to stream their entertainment options. Acknowledging this generational gap and wanting to author a tome that reflects the current state of affairs in academia, I am proud to be joined in writing this book by a current graduate student, Catalina Flores.

Throughout this book, you will find stories by our friends and colleagues that describe their unique journeys in becoming I-O professionals. Here, in the Preface, Catalina and I will share our own stories, which may help you understand our motivation in creating this book.

Dennis Doverspike
To be honest, I never set out to be an I-O Psychologist. Even now, in my eyes, I am a psychologist first, who happens to have I-O Psychology as a specialty area.

My guess would be very few children grow up wanting to be I-O Psychologists or dress up as I-O Psychologists for Halloween. Thinking back, my first dream was to be an astronaut; a dream which was squashed when I had to start wearing glasses in about 5th grade. The next occupation I can remember considering was that of oceanographer, marine biologist (yes, like George Costanza from *Seinfeld*), or marine engineer. My hopes of living underwater disappeared when I went to college at a university that lacked an engineering major and was far from any oceans. Next, I considered medicine but a lack of studying fortitude caused me to look for other options. At this point, I reasoned that if I could not explore outer space, or underwater, I would venture inner space, into an understanding of the psychology of the mind. So, in college, I became a psychology major. Well, that and I spent too much time in the college ratskeller and when I took my first Introduction to Psychology course I earned an "A;" serendipity has shaped much of my career.

When I had to apply for graduate school I was incredibly naïve, a state I hope this book helps some of you avoid. As a result, I ended up in a master's program in clinical psychology. One of my clinical professors suggested that I would be better off in an I-O Program, and so for my Ph.D., I did switch to I-O Psychology.

Proudly, I attended and then completed in four years the Ph.D. program at The University of Akron. During that time, I had a number of eminent teachers, including Gerald Barrett, Ralph Alexander, and Robert Lord.

You may start to sense a pattern here, but when I finished my Ph.D., I still had no idea what I wanted to do, or what I was doing, and so I applied for jobs in industry, consulting, and academia. I was offered jobs in all three and decided to take a job with the Psychology Department and Ph.D. program at The University of Nebraska at Omaha.

After two years at Omaha, where I met a number of now lifelong friends, I was offered the opportunity to return to The University of Akron. That was back in 1984. I am still at Akron, except now I am in a new career stage, reducing my workload toward retirement.

As an academic, I have been somewhat fortunate, and also unique, in that over the years I have always maintained an active consulting practice. At both Omaha and Akron, I ran university-based consulting centers. In addition, I have consulted for other firms and for myself. My consulting contacts range from the U.S. Federal Government to small cities, from large international organizations to small family owned businesses, and from large to one-person consulting firms. In addition, I have been active as an expert witness in court cases. In one of the accomplishments of which I am proudest, working with Winfred Arthur of Texas A&M University we created a cognitive ability test and a personality assessment that have been administered to over 5 million job applicants.

My career has been long and fulfilling. Now, I am happy to try to share my experiences with you as your start your journey. Although, sometimes I still look to the stars and wish I could have been an astronaut.

Catalina Flores

I also did not dream of being an I-O Psychologist as a child; instead, according to my parents, from a young age I declared that I wanted to be a judge. If I had to guess, their avid watching of true crime television was responsible for my early drive to bring the bad guys to justice. Furthering this drive, as a child, my dad would take me to the courthouse to watch the trials in action. Although later my aspirations for judgeship faded, I still thought I might like to be a lawyer.

Going into my senior year of high school, we were asked to choose one social studies elective. Although Government and Politics course was the obvious choice, I was also drawn to psychology because I thought regardless of your career it would be helpful to have an understanding of human behavior (and the minds of criminals, of course). I could not decide between the two courses, so I got special permission from the department chair and was able to take both. I'm thankful that I was able to do so because I ended up enjoying the Psychology course much more, and it was that experience that led me down this path of becoming an I-O Psychologist.

I always imagined that a career in psychology would involve counseling patients, which I did not think would be a good fit for me. However, my misconception changed when I learned about I-O Psychology in the course. My teacher showed a clear enthusiasm for the field and described it as an exciting and lucrative career opportunity. It turns out her daughter was an I-O practitioner, so we heard stories about her different consulting projects, which illustrated how psychology can be used to solve problems at work. Soon enough I was sold on the field, giving up my childhood dream to fight crime, and deciding to pursue I-O as a specialty option.

I went on to major in I-O Psychology at the Zicklin School of Business in the Macaulay Honors program at Baruch College, City University of New York (CUNY). My education at Baruch College was unusual in that it is one of the few places where there is an undergraduate I-O major offered. This major gave me a background in business and psychology coursework, in addition to focused upper-level

I-O courses. Through my major and experiences as a research assistant, I learned more about I-O and became intrinsically committed to the choice I made as a high school student when I had little actual knowledge of the field.

In my senior year of college, I applied to M.A./Ph.D. programs in I-O Psychology and found a great fit at The University of Akron. Throughout my time at Akron so far, I have learned from and collaborated with several faculty members and graduate students. In particular, Joelle Elicker and Dennis Doverspike have consistently challenged me to pursue different opportunities, encouraged and affirmed my thinking outside of the box, and have provided candid feedback and career advice. While most of my peers have a clear picture of whether they want an applied or academic career, I am still not sure what my dream job would look like. I have enjoyed trying out teaching, research, and consulting projects, and I plan to continue gaining a wide range of experiences while I am still in graduate school in the hope that things will become clear to me along the way.

Although I am still at a very early stage in my career, I would not have even had the confidence to apply to doctoral programs without guidance and advice from CUNY faculty and graduate students. I try to pay it forward by maintaining relationships with undergraduate students who may be interested in I-O. By sharing my own stories, connecting students with research opportunities, and helping with graduate school applications, I feel I can make a difference by exposing people to a field they may not have thought of, that could end up being a great match.

PART 1

BEGINNING THOUGHTS

CHAPTER 1

Introduction

So, you want to be an Industrial-Organizational (I-O) Psychologist. Congratulations on your choice of a prospective career and thank you for picking up this book. With the right combination of motivation and career guidance, you should be able to attain your goal. This book has been written to assist you with the academic and career choices you will need to make in order to obtain the education and experience required to gain entry into the I-O profession. Starting with what you will need to think about as an undergraduate, we take you through a series of steps that finishes with choosing specific specialty areas within I-O Psychology.

On the day you begin work as an I-O Psychologist, we are confident you will find it to be an exciting, dynamic, and enriching profession.

WHAT IS I-O PSYCHOLOGY?

You probably already know that psychology is the "study of the mind and behavior." I-O Psychology then is the study of behavior in the workplace, including 1) the analysis of jobs, people, and organizations; 2) the measurement of behaviors and mental processes related to the workplace; 3) the development of interventions and training aimed at improving job performance and satisfaction; and 4) the evaluation of our work to determine whether we are really making a difference in job and organizational performance.

Psychologists are those professionals who study the mind and behavior. Psychologists are sometimes categorized into heath care providers (primarily clinical and counseling psychologists), basic researchers (most of whom are academics), and general applied psychologists. I-O

Psychologists would fall under the category of the latter. Chapter 2, and really the book as a whole, attempts to provide you with an answer to the questions of "What is I-O Psychology and what does an I-O Psychologist do?"

HOW DO I BECOME AN I-O PSYCHOLOGIST?

Typically, to get a job as an I-O Psychologist, you need to obtain at least a master's degree. Of course, to obtain a master's degree you have to apply for and be admitted to graduate school after completing a bachelor's degree. Part 2 of this book discusses the undergraduate years, beginning with Chapter 3, which covers what you should be thinking about as an undergraduate if this is a possibility for you. The process of applying to graduate school and making decisions with regard to where to attend can be an adventure in and of itself and are covered in Chapters 4, 5, and 6.

Once you are admitted and choose your graduate program, you can look forward to anywhere from two to as many as six years of graduate study (and sometimes even longer), which is the topic of Part 3 on the graduate years. Fortunately, graduate school can be an exciting time and you will probably never know more about psychology and statistics than you will know in that stage of your career. Chapter 7 discusses the graduate school experience, including how to be successful and relatively happy.

Prior to applying for full-time employment, many individuals pursue an internship, which allows students to gain supervised, structured experience in the field. Fortunately, there are many internship options for those interested in I-O; however, the experience of applying for and completing a developmental internship can still be a challenging one. We offer our advice in Chapter 8.

In most states, an individual must be licensed as a psychologist to use the title "Psychologist" or "I-O Psychologist." However, many I-O Psychologists are opposed to licensure and the licensure requirement is a controversial one. In Chapter 9, we discuss licensure, and offer our views on this hotly debated topic.

Many individuals may not decide to pursue graduate study in I-O right out of college. Some people may choose to become clinical or counseling psychologists for example, and then decide after a few years that providing therapy is not what they want to do every day. Chapter 10 is for those individuals who would like to transition into I-O Psychology from either a totally different career area or from a different psychological specialty.

HOW DO I FIND A JOB?

You have walked across the stage and received your diploma, completed an internship, and now you need to find a job. As you celebrate, you cannot help but worry about what the future might hold. Will you land your dream job? How do you get started with your job search? What types of employers should you consider?

In Part 4 of this book, Chapters 11 through 14, we discuss how to find a job and begin a career in various sectors of I-O Psychology. We use the term "sector" to correspond to different types of employers. The sectors are academic (Chapter 11), consulting (Chapter 12), industry (Chapter 13), and government (Chapter 14). For each sector, we review how to look for jobs, when and how to apply, how to present yourself, and what to expect during recruitment and onboarding. Wrapping up, we offer final thoughts in Part 5, Chapter 15.

WHO SHOULD READ THIS BOOK?

In writing this book, we hoped to make it applicable for a wide, diverse audience. Although primarily oriented toward readers in the United States, most graduate programs receive applicants from many different countries. Whether you are a high school student considering a college major, an undergraduate curious about graduate school, a first-year graduate student adjusting to life in academe, or a midcareer psychologist considering transitioning into I-O Psychology, we have tried to provide information and content that will help to meet your needs in making your educational and career decisions.

We also envision that this book could be used as a supplement to other textbooks in an undergraduate I-O Psychology class. For those schools that offer a Careers in Psychology course, this book could serve as supplemental reading.

ONLINE MATERIALS

We would be the first to admit that there is a wealth of material that can be found online. YouTube, for example, has a plethora of videos on the topic of becoming an I-O Psychologist. There are several excellent blogs covering different I-O topics as well. In this book, our approach to online materials has been to mention websites where material can be found, especially the Society for Industrial and Organizational Psychology site (also known as SIOP or Division 14), but not to provide links that might change. If you are interested in following up on researching any of the online materials mentioned in this book, you can simply Google the topic, ask Siri, Alexa, or Google Assistant.

TEXTBOX 1.1 YOUTUBE

Go to YouTube and type in "Industrial Organizational Psychologist." You will be amazed at how many videos you find there. You could probably spend a year just watching all the videos, something we do not recommend.

CAREER VIGNETTES

TEXTBOX 1.2 AN OLD JOKE RECYCLED

I saw a college student walk into the Career Guidance Office at the University and tell the guidance counselor, "I do not know what I want to do with my life, I am a psychology major and I am so confused." The guidance counselor places three objects on the table – a cute little mouse, a stack of Rorschach inkblot cards, and a stack of dollar bills. The counselor says to the student "Pick one." Now, unbeknownst to the student, this is a simple vocational test. If the student picks the mouse, the student will become an experimental psychologist. If the student picks the Rorschach cards, the student will become a clinical psychologist. If the student picks the stack of money, the student will quit psychology and go into a career as a salesperson. The poor undecided student pauses for a second and then picks all three. The guidance counselor quickly says, "Better get ready to apply for graduate school, someday you will be a successful Industrial-Organizational Psychologist."

To help to illustrate the points made in the book, we asked friends and colleagues to contribute their stories with regard to becoming an I-O Psychologist. Those stories appear in chapters throughout the book, with our own stories appearing in the Preface.

Career vignettes were provided by:

- Matt O'Connell, Ph.D. was Co-Founder and Executive Vice President of Select International and now has started a second career as an author of fictional, historical novels (Chapter 2).
- Kate Ferguson is currently an undergraduate at The University of Akron (Chapter 3).

- Cheryl Hardy is currently an undergraduate at The University of Akron (Chapter 3).
- Ketaki Sodhi, M.A. is a Ph.D. student at The University of Akron (Chapter 4).
- Eric S. Hutchison, M.B.A., M.S. is a Ph.D. candidate at Walden University and works in the public sector (Chapter 5).
- Russell Steiner is currently an M.A./Ph. D. student at The University of Akron (Chapter 6).
- Katya Caravella, M.A. is a graduate of The University of Akron and a Human Resource (HR) Project Specialist at Northwood Investors, LLC in Colorado (Chapter 7).
- Tyler Slezak, M.A. is a Ph.D. candidate at The University of Akron and an Innovation Intern at Shaker International (Chapter 8).
- Brodie Gregory Riordan, Ph.D. is a graduate of The University of Akron and is currently a Manager in Partner Learning and Development at McKinsey & Company (Chapter 9).
- Ernest Hoffman, Ph.D. is a graduate of The University of Akron and works as a Senior Management Consultant at PRADCO, Columbus, OH (Chapter 10).
- Alexandra I. Zelin, Ph.D. is a graduate of The University of Akron and is an Assistant Professor of I-O Psychology at The University of Tennessee at Chattanooga (Chapter 11).
- Jacqueline Carpenter, Ph.D. is a graduate of The University of Akron and is currently a consultant with Shaker International, Cleveland, OH (Chapter 12).
- Andrew (Drew) Lam, Ph.D. is a graduate of The University of Akron and the Senior Manager of Organization Development at Shearer's Snacks (Chapter 13).
- Gina Seaton, Ph.D. is a graduate of The University of Akron and serves as Global Talent Assessment and Development Manager with PepsiCo (Chapter 13).
- George Vaughn, M.A. is a Manager of Employment Testing at the Cuyahoga Country Personnel Review Commission, Cleveland, OH (Chapter 14).

ABOUT THE AUTHORS

Of course, you may be curious as to who we are and what gives our opinions any credibility. Let us introduce ourselves.

Dennis Doverspike, Ph.D., ABPP, is the President of Doverspike Consulting, LLC. He formerly held the title of Full Professor of

Psychology at The University of Akron, Senior Fellow of the Institute for Life-Span Development and Gerontology, and Director of the Center for Organizational Research. He is certified as a specialist in Industrial-Organizational Psychology and in Organizational and Business Consulting by the American Board of Professional Psychology (ABPP) and is a licensed psychologist in the State of Ohio. Dr. Doverspike has over 40 years of experience working with consulting firms and with public and private sector organizations. He is the author of three books and over 200 other professional publications. Dennis Doverspike received his Ph.D. in Psychology in 1983 from The University of Akron. He has taught courses at both the graduate and undergraduate levels, and directed dissertations, theses, and practica.

Catalina Flores, M.A., is a Ph.D. candidate in Industrial-Organizational Psychology at The University of Akron. Her research interests are in diversity in the workplace, employee selection, and performance management. She has taught undergraduate courses in Psychology and Statistics, and served as Managing Director for the Center for Organizational Research (COR), a consulting center at The University of Akron for two years prior to beginning an internship at Shaker International. During her time working for COR she has gained experience managing a variety of hands-on projects with organizations across multiple industries, in the areas of selection, employee surveys, and statistical analysis.

ACKNOWLEDGEMENTS

We would like to acknowledge the people who have helped us make this book a reality. Our career vignette contributors were integral to our vision of highlighting the many twists and turns in becoming an I-O Psychologist and we are thankful that they were willing to share their stories. We also want to thank the faculty, staff, graduate students, and alumni of The University of Akron who have served as a sounding board and source of support throughout this process. At Taylor & Francis, we would like to thank our editor, Julie Toich, and Christina Chronister, who encouraged us to consider authoring the book. We also want to thank the copy-editor Melanie Marshall.

CHAPTER 2

The I-O Psychologist

Amazingly, almost every year there is at least one student who enters the graduate program at The University of Akron who has no idea what an I-O Psychologist is or does. Sometimes that student finds out what an I-O Psychologist is and leaves, and other times that student goes on to become a famous I-O Psychologist. Every year in our first-year class, there are several I-O students who have some idea what an I-O Psychologist is but have never taken an I-O class, and there is even the occasional student who was never a psychology major. So, if you are thinking about a career in I-O but do not really know what an I-O Psychologist does, do not despair, for yours is far from an unusual case. We have written this chapter for you. In this chapter, we will provide answers to:

- What is an I-O Psychologist?
- What does an I-O Psychologist do?
- Where, or in what sectors, do I-O Psychologists work?
- What can I expect in terms of job opportunities and pay?

WHAT IS AN I-O PSYCHOLOGIST?

If we were to run into someone in an elevator and they asked, *What does an I-O Psychologist do?* we would likely reply, *they apply psychology to the workplace*, or perhaps, *they study human behavior in the workplace*. The American Psychological Association (APA) (2010) provide the definition that it is ... characterized by the scientific study of human behavior in organizations and the work place... focuses on deriving principles of individual, group and organizational behavior and applying this knowledge to the solution of problems at work. The Society for Industrial and

Organizational Psychology (SIOP) offers as a definition for the public that the field tries to understand and measure human behavior to improve employees' satisfaction in their work, employers' ability to select and promote the best people, and to generally make the workplace better for the men and women who work there.

We would not disagree with the above definitions, however, in the Introduction we have presented our definition that an I-O Psychologist studies behavior in the workplace, including: 1) the analysis of jobs, people, and organizations; 2) the measurement of behaviors and mental processes related to the workplace; 3) the development of interventions and training aimed at improving job performance and satisfaction; and 4) the evaluation of our work to determine whether we are really making a difference in job and organizational performance. We like our own definition because it builds on the four critical functions performed by a psychologist: analysis and problem identification, testing and measurement, intervention, and evaluation. However, any single definition fails to capture the complexity or scope of the activities performed by an I-O Psychologist.

Since the beginning of the field, there has been an invisible but recognizable divide between those who identify as scientists and those who identify as practitioners. Presently, the annual SIOP conference has become a place in which I-O Psychologists of different backgrounds discuss and debate the scientist-practitioner divide and work toward lessening that gap. The "scientists" are those who produce I-O knowledge, usually found in academia, in either psychology departments or business schools. The "practitioners" are those whose work is in applying I-O knowledge, and can be found in "real-world" settings, including consulting, industry, health care, and government.

Operationally, most I-O Psychologists either have a master's or Ph.D. related to I-O Psychology, or have a job that carries with it the title of "I-O Psychologist." There are many related occupations, including human resource specialists, organizational consultants, consulting psychologists, human factors psychologists, and other types of general applied psychologists. Unlike clinical and other types of health care psychology, most I-O Psychologists are not licensed, so licensure or certification cannot be used as a clear indicator and, as a result, I-O Psychologists may work under a variety of job titles. We have provided a sample list of frequently encountered titles in Table 2.1.

So, what constitutes an I-O Psychologist is a fuzzy category, other than the person self-identifies as an I-O Psychologist. Many I-O Psychologists can also be identified by their membership in the professional society, SIOP.

Table 2.1 List of Sample Job Titles

Industry

- Industrial-Organizational Psychologist
- Vice President of Human Resources
- Personnel Psychologist
- Personnel Specialist
- Director of Organizational Development
- Manager of Employee Relations
- Talent Management Associate
- Director of Training and Development
- Compensation Manager

Consulting

- Principal Consultant
- Associate Consultant
- Human Resource Consultant
- Senior Consultant
- Organizational Development Consultant
- Leadership Consultant
- Industrial-Organizational Intern
- Consulting Psychologist
- Executive Coach
- Leadership Coach

Government

- Assessment Specialist
- Selection Team Leader
- Manager of Testing Programs
- Director of Merit Systems and Programs
- Human Factors Leader
- Director of Psychological Research
- Human Performance Laboratory Director
- Researcher

Academic

- Dean
- Department Head
- Full Professor
- Associate Professor
- Assistant Professor
- Director of Organizational Research Center

TEXTBOX 2.1 THE SIOP WEBSITE

There are several great sources of information for what an I-O Psychologist does. One of the best places to start is with the organization that serves as the primary professional home for I-O Psychologists, which is the Society for Industrial and Organizational Psychology (SIOP) or Division 14 of the American Psychological Association. At the SIOP website (www.siop.org/), you will also find sections devoted to other important topics including graduate study, salaries, and the competencies required for different career sectors or paths.

TEXTBOX 2.2 O*NET

A valuable source of information is the U.S. Federal Government's, O*NET. Go to the O*NET webpage and type in "Industrial-Organizational Psychologist." This will take you to a page with a treasure trove of data and information on what it is that I-O Psychologists do.

WHAT DOES AN I-O PSYCHOLOGIST DO?

Historically, I-O Psychology is one of the oldest recognized specialties in the field of psychology. The roots of the profession go back to the early 1900s, to pioneers such as Walter Dill Scott, who was interested in psychology applied to advertising, and Hugo Münsterberg. Münsterberg authored two of the first textbooks and helped to define the field as including: 1) selecting the best employees; 2) designing jobs so as to obtain the highest performance and most satisfied workers; and 3) maximizing the potential of the hired employees through training and performance management.

In our view, a major turning point in the history of I-O Psychology occurred around 1978. The 1977–1980 period was important for many reasons, including the introduction of meta-analysis, the switch from an underlying behaviorist approach to a social-cognitive one, and a technological revolution with the introduction of the first personal computers including the Apple II and the Commodore PET. However, the most significant event for I-O Psychology was the release in 1978 of the *Uniform Guidelines on Employee Selection Procedures* by the U.S. Government. This document can be seen as creating a full employment act for I-O Psychology. In combination with other factors, there was a sudden explosion in the number of I-O graduate programs, the number of students in graduate school, and the availability of jobs for I-O

Psychologists as a result of the *Guidelines*. Due to the nature of the *Guidelines*, the jobs created were those that dealt most specifically with assessment or testing.

I-O Psychologists do many things, but one of the driving factors in the I-O boom has been the need for professionals to develop and validate selection procedures for organizations that comply with legal requirements. Thus, while we will discuss other activities performed by I-O Psychologists, perhaps the unique, identifying feature is the role played in the assessment, testing, and selection of employees.

However, I-O Psychology is a broad field and I-O Psychologists do much more than testing and selection. Returning to the concepts of Münsterberg, many people are attracted to I-O Psychology because they see it as an opportunity to make a difference by improving organizations and society. Others want to take a broad approach to wellness by considering how work satisfaction influences overall life satisfaction. Then there are mid-career individuals who have been in the workplace, where they may have encountered abusive supervisors or dysfunctional organizations. As a result, these individuals find themselves searching for answers and believe the solutions may lie in the approaches and methods of I-O Psychology, especially theories of positive psychology, humanistic organizations, and work-life balance.

As the name suggests, one division is between industrial, probably an outdated title, and organizational. A focus on the industrial side, also sometimes referred to as a micro-focus, suggests the primary work activities include job analysis, recruitment, testing, selection, motivation, and training. A focus on the organizational side, also sometimes referred to as a macro-focus, suggests the primary work activities include motivation, leadership, diversity, organizational development, and work-life balance.

Thus, most I-O Psychologists not only see themselves as either a "scientist" or "practitioner," but also either "I" or "O" focused. In Table 2.2, we call out some more specific areas of research within I and O sides that form the basis of I-O knowledge and practice. We encourage you to think about these topics and consider which side you are more drawn to. From the practitioner perspective, an attempt to chronicle all the possible activities that I-O Psychologists engage in would take more pages than we have available, but Table 2.3 provides a list of some of the activities I-O Psychologists perform.

In Table 2.4, you will find our first career vignette, which is Matt O'Connell's telling of his personal adventures in I-O. We start with Matt because of the varied nature of his experience; we hope you enjoy his story.

Table 2.2 Partial List of I-O Research Areas

Industrial Psychology

- Psychometrics/testing (e.g., reliability, validity)
- Personnel selection
- Legal issues
- Test bias and fairness
- Interviews
- Assessments and predicting performance
- Recruitment
- Training
- Feedback and performance appraisal
- Employee development
- Coaching

Organizational Psychology

- Job design
- Job attitudes (e.g., satisfaction, engagement)
- Groups and teams
- Organizational development
- Organizational culture and climate
- Social exchange and trust
- Motivation
- Leadership
- Diversity
- Stress and well-being
- Work-life balance

Table 2.3 Partial List of I-O Practitioner Activities

- Job analysis
- Job evaluation
- Developing assessment tools for selection/placement/classification
- The validation of test instruments consistent with legal and professional standards and guidelines
- Individual psychological assessment
- Development of recruitment materials, websites, and programs
- Providing services as an expert witness in employment-related cases
- Developing performance management and appraisal systems
- Identifying training and development needs, including need analysis
- Program evaluation
- Succession and workforce planning
- Creating and developing talent management systems
- Executive and managerial coaching
- Career coaching

- Providing supervision to organizational psychologists or human resource professionals
- Managing human resource units or other organizational psychologists
- Applying psychology in management
- Organizational change and development
- Job design and redesign
- Process consultation
- Attitude survey management
- Designing and undertaking organizational interventions
- Team building
- Maximizing the effectiveness of work groups and organizations
- Assessing needs and facilitating organization change
- Providing consultation during mergers and acquisitions
- Dealing with aggression, violence, harassment

Table 2.4 Matt O'Connell, Ph.D., the Journey of a Global I-O Psychologist and Novelist

If you would have asked me when I was 19 years old, I would have said, without hesitation, that I wanted to be an orthopedic surgeon. But after visiting a few hospitals, talking with a few doctors, I realized that was not what I wanted to do at all. So, I was left trying to figure out what to do. At some point, I talked with two psychologists that lived down the road from me and they suggested that I consider I-O Psychology. That was before my junior year in college, and I honestly had no idea what I-O Psychologists did. My college did not offer any courses in I-O and none of the psychology professors knew that much about the field either. But, after reading a little bit more about the field I thought I had to give it a shot. That is about the level of research I did before applying to and ultimately attending graduate school.

Early in my I-O career, I had the great fortune of working with some true giants in the field. In graduate school I was able to study under Ralph Alexander, who was my thesis advisor. After finishing my thesis on Item Response Theory back in 1988, Ralph presented me with an article that he had ripped out of *American Statistician* about binomial spleens. Ralph said that he thought this would be a good idea for a dissertation. Considering that I had spent the past six months wading my way through journals such as *Psychometrika*, with more Greek letters on the page than English words, I took a big gulp and told Ralph that I thought my talents were best suited for something more applied. I was afraid that he would try and convince me to move forward with the project. But Ralph, being the gracious man he was, said that was no problem and he wished me nothing but luck. After that, I switched advisors to Dennis Doverspike and did a dissertation on self-directed work teams.

I have worked closely with Dennis for more than 25 years, have published several professional articles with him, and consider him a close friend and mentor.

I also had the opportunity to study under and to also work for Gerald Barrett. I still draw on many of the lessons I learned under Jerry about legal defensibility in consulting to this day, more than 27 years since I took my last class. I have sat across from the OFCCP's top psychologist and defended our tests and selection processes with the confidence that I gained through the training I received, in large part, from Dr. Barrett.

After leaving The University of Akron's graduate program, I worked for DDI as a consultant, and then ultimately as a senior consultant. While there, I had the opportunity to actually design assessment centers with true pioneers in that field including Doug Bray, Ann Howard, and Bill Byham. I remember sitting in a brainstorming session for a new assessment center with Doug and Ann and, as a 25 year old consultant, thinking to myself that this was pretty rarified air. I learned a lot about how to build assessments, how to manage projects and interact with clients. I spent three and a half years there and left with a lot of fond memories.

At some point I decided that I wanted to try it on my own. At DDI, I was positioned to be in charge of implementing a new computer-based assessment. It was 1993 and computer-based assessments were relatively new. I wanted to do some very creative things with simulations and different item types, but DDI really wanted to just put some of their paper-and-pencil tests on the computer. It was by no means a bad business decision on their part, but I was not excited about it. As such, I decided that if there ever was a time to give it a shot, it was then.

On August 1, 1993, I sat in a small office in my house in Pittsburgh and Select International, Inc. was born. I was determined to do this on my own and not borrow anything from DDI. I did not try and take one of their assessments and customize it. In fact, I made a point of throwing out anything that I had from DDI related to assessments. The only thing I kept were Thornton and Byham's book *Assessment Centers and Managerial Performance* and a few other similar books. I did not even want to have the temptation to fall back on using something of theirs and I definitely never wanted to be accused of plagiarizing their intellectual property.

At that time, on the heels of Barrick and Mount's (1991) meta-analysis, there was a lot of momentum regarding the resurgence of personality inventories and the emergence of the five-factor model (FFM). I started studying in earnest to understand all I could about which personality factors best predicted performance. I was also very interested in situational judgment tests (SJTs) as well as trying to create shorter, more focused interactive assessments. Based on my experiences with a wide range of assessments, I was convinced that I could get more out of three, ten-minute assessments than one 30-minute one.

I secured a deal with a Mexican department store chain that would allow me to design a new assessment solution, as well as provide outsourcing for those positions. From my perspective, it was a perfect opportunity. I would have free rein in determining what assessments to use, and I would see how it worked first hand. There were obviously a number of challenges. I did not have any tests, I did not know how to program a computer, and I did not speak Spanish. I also did not have a lot of money to hire people to do any of those things. Other than that, it was a perfect situation.

I set out and took courses in a programming language that was predominately used for computer-based training, but which I was convinced could be used for testing. I had a friend of mine create an applicant tracking system that would score the tests, store the item-level data, and create reports. The next year I taught myself how to program in FoxPro and rewrote the system myself. I wrote new personality scales, SJTs, and interactive simulations for our first assessment, which was targeted at retail salespeople. After about six months of writing tests, creating code, doing job analyses, and preparing everything in Mexico, my wife and I packed up our Jeep and drove to Guadalajara.

I spent a little over two years in Mexico. We had a lot of success there. By the time we moved back to the U.S. in March 1996, Select International's assessments were being used for hiring salespeople, supervisors and managers at over 50 stores throughout Mexico, including the two largest retail chains, Liverpool and Sears. Select International had 20 employees, an office in Guadalajara, as well as one in Monterrey, Mexico. We conducted six validation studies with good results. I also learned to speak Spanish fairly fluently, which was a plus.

While I was in Mexico I became interested in transformational leadership and reached out to Bruce Avolio, who was also an Akron graduate. At that time, the internet was in its infancy and we mostly communicated by long faxes and eventually through AOL. Bruce was gracious enough to work with a person whom he had never met and shared a lot of his expertise and insights with me, as well as access to his MLQ 360 scale. I worked with Bruce for the next three years and we not only developed and validated an SJT ethical reasoning scale based on Kohlberg's moral development theory, we also created an in-basket that evaluated the core transformational and transactional leadership competencies. We used that in-basket and the ethical reasoning assessment with great success for several years with a wide range of companies in the U.S., Mexico, and South Africa.

When I came back to the U.S., two partners, Kevin and Chris Klinvex, joined me and we started expanding in the U.S., Mexico, and the world. This year marks Select International's 25th anniversary. A lot of things, including two major recessions and the rise and fall of the dot-com boom, have happened over that time period. Select International now employs just over 100 full-time employees. Not including me, we have ten Ph.D. level I-O psychologists and 14 at the M.A. level. We have a wide range of assessment solutions that cover a broad range of positions and industries, including manufacturing, call centers, service/retail, safety, and health care. A conservative count would indicate that we have over 50 unique assessment solutions, and within them there are typically anywhere from five to 30 variations. It is not an exaggeration to say that we have over 200 different complete assessments. We have a dedicated R&D team as well as a 20-person software development group. All of these assessments were developed internally and are proprietary to Select International. As director of R&D, I was involved in the development of every assessment we created, until I stepped down from that position four years ago. On average we have grown by at least 20% per year for the past 25 years and successfully compete head to head with the largest assessment providers in the world.

We work with nearly 400 firms, many of whom are Global 1000 firms. We conduct approximately 8,000 assessments per day, 365 days a year in over 20 languages and over 80 countries. While we work with clients who are covered by the EEOC and, in some cases, the OFCCP, because we adhere to the highest professional standards, no client of Select International has ever lost a defense of their selection process. This is something we are very committed to upholding and of which we are very proud.

Two of the things I am most proud of are our continued commitment to conducting applied research, as well as winning or finishing as finalist in "Best Companies to Work for" in Pittsburgh, multiple times. I have always found that staying active in research is not only intellectually stimulating, but it also helps us develop better solutions for our clients. Our people feel the same way and are encouraged to form relationships with academic institutions, get involved in SIOP, and continue to conduct and publish applied research.

Not surprisingly, my research interests predominately focus on areas that relate to applied issues, primarily related to assessment and selection. I have worked closely with Rich Griffith from the Florida Institute of Technology on trying to better understand, identify, and correct for applicant faking. I have also turned my attention to better identify people who are more likely to be involved in safety incidents as well as creating a way for everyone to gain insights about their safety DNA and reduce their risk. The results we have obtained to date have been very impressive and we continue to develop and improve our solutions. Currently, our safety assessments are used widely in the energy, construction, manufacturing, and mining industries. Our SafetyDNA® program won the 2017 new product of the year award for best online safety training program from Occupational Safety & Health. One of the really rewarding things about working with safety is that our tools and solutions impact people's lives. They make them safer.

In addition to serving a more strategic role in helping to guide our business to greater heights, a good deal of my time is spent writing white papers and business outcome reports which help educate our consultants and our clients on key issues.

Separate from anything I-O related, in the past several years, I have shifted my primary focus to writing fiction. I published my first novel, *The Painter of Time*, in 2015, and my second, *Spirit of the Fox*, in 2018. One deals with art history and the other with spirit possession; two topics that are pretty far from say, comparing the efficacy of various tools for identifying faking in self-report measures. Obviously, it is very different than writing technical articles. But, it is one of the most intellectually stimulating things I have ever done. I hope to continue writing fiction until I cannot write any longer.

Given the extremely limited knowledge I had coming into the field of I-O, I cannot imagine choosing a better career. It has provided me with exceptional flexibility, intellectual stimulation, and the opportunity to test out our theories and refine our tools based on real world results. I could not ask for anything more.

WHERE DO I-O PSYCHOLOGISTS WORK?

As mentioned in the previous section, the activities performed by I-O Psychologists vary greatly by the area, career path, or sector where the individual is employed. Adopting the approach used by SIOP, the four sectors (and the approximate percentage of I-O Psychologists in each in parentheses) are:

1. Academic (40%)
2. Consulting (25%)
3. Industry (25%)
4. Government (10%)

Sample job titles within each sector are presented in Table 2.1.

In general, and across sectors, upon initial hiring and entry into the organization, the new employee starts in the role of an individual contributor. As individuals gain expertise and experience, they are faced with a fork in the career road. They can move into a role where they supervise other staff and professionals as a manager or they can continue functioning as a thought leader or expert individual contributor. With management, it is possible to continue to advance into higher-level managerial and executive roles.

1. *Academic*

Being in an academic environment means that you will be teaching others. It is safe to say, not everyone is cut out for teaching. Most jobs in higher level education require not only teaching, but also service, research, and publication. Positions at top schools require significant amounts of research and publication, the dreaded publish-or-perish model, as well as the ability to bring in grants to fund your own research work.

There are several choices to be made among the many job types in academia. You can go to a community college, a four-year college, a university with master's degree offerings, or a university that has a Ph.D. graduate program. There are traditional schools and online schools, so you can even work at a distance. You can work as a full-time tenure-track professor, or as an adjunct, or part-time faculty member teaching a few evening courses as a supplement to work in another practice. The minimum qualification is usually a Ph.D., but there may be limited job openings for individuals with the master's degree.

As in the other sectors, the professional in an academic setting may pursue positions involving supervisory responsibilities or remain more independent. For those who wish to remain an individual contributor the typical career path is assistant professor, associate professor, and then full professor. For those interested in management, the progression would be some professor title, department head, dean, provost, and, ultimately, president of a university.

2.   *Consulting*

If you want to be a consultant, you can hang out your own shingle (i.e., start your own practice), join a small, boutique consulting firm, or become an employee of a large, global organization. Consulting firms can also be dichotomized into those that concentrate on the private sector versus those that primarily work with public sector agencies or the government. The minimum qualification is usually a master's degree, with a Ph.D. preferred in some instances.

There tend to be three main tracks pursued. Individual contributors can be divided into those that work primarily on projects with clients and those that work primarily on research projects with minimal client contact. Then, there are those who seek out managerial roles. Regardless of the type of employer, a consultant has to bring in billable work (i.e., stay green by charging a client for your time). Thus, consultants often work long days and long weeks, and depending on the degree of client contact, there may also be a lot of travel involved.

3.   *Industry*

The term "industry" is old-fashioned and outdated, but we will use it as it reflects standard terminology. By industry, we mean private sector companies, which includes a wide spectrum of companies such as health care, information technology, retail, and, of course, good old manufacturing. Industry is often seen as involving internal consulting. The minimum qualification is usually a master's degree, with somewhat more limited roles available for those with Ph.Ds.

I-O professionals usually take on either the role of a specialist in some domain, like training and development, or function as more of a human resource generalist. As with the other areas, the individual I-O Psychologist may seek promotions into management positions, or prefer to remain an individual contributor, as an advanced specialist. Internal consultants have the benefit of seeing the results of their work within the organization, compared to consulting in which client work tends to be more project-based.

4.   *Government*

Government also covers a broad area including federal, state, and local, various government agencies, and even the military. The minimum qualification is usually a master's degree. However, a unique feature of the government is that formal degree attainment has often been deemphasized. As a result, it is not unusual to find someone with a high school degree occupying a position with significant responsibility for traditional I-O functions.

Another unique feature of government is that even when moving into managerial roles, employees are often expected to spend a significant amount of time on project delivery, research, or serving as a technical expert. Unique job titles are often another feature of government employment. Nevertheless, individuals still tend to follow either an expert individual contributor or a managerial path.

WHAT CAN I EXPECT IN TERMS OF JOB OPPORTUNITIES AND PAY?

I-O Psychology has recently become a media darling in terms of predictions of future job growth. Multiple media outlets have identified I-O Psychology as one of the hot jobs of the future; one where demand will outstrip supply.

We see no reason to question this optimistic view of the future for I-O. Despite the existence of a number of online and professional schools training a large number of practitioners, the supply of trained I-O Psychologists should remain limited. The most recent data we could find from the American Psychological Association reports that about 130 doctorates were awarded per year. While supply should remain steady, demand should increase due to 1) the seemingly insatiable appetite of employers for online preemployment assessments, and 2) the increased realization by organizations of the importance of a psychologically healthy workforce. Thus, we would agree with the media forecasts that there will be a clear future need for individuals with master's and doctorates in I-O Psychology.

Unfortunately, this demand does not always translate into competitive compensation. Still, the salary ranges for I-O Psychologists are certainly higher than those for many other areas of psychology and the salaries are on an upward or rising trend. According to a recent salary study done by SIOP, the median salary for those with a master's degree is $85,000, and the median salary for those with a doctorate is $120,000. Over the last several years, the difference in median income has been about a 40% higher salary for those with doctorates compared to master's degrees. We should note here that all salaries are in 2018 U.S. dollars.

Of course, those are average salaries and individual salaries can vary quite a bit. Pay will be higher with experience and tenure, and depend strongly on the sector, location, and cost of living. Starting salaries can be expected to be much lower than quoted average salaries.

Even within a sector, salaries can vary greatly. For example, if upon graduation you were to look at entry level teaching jobs in community colleges, you might expect a salary in the $45,000 to $55,000 range for nine months. Even at a top I-O program, you might be lucky to be offered a salary in the $70,000 to $80,000. However, if you are in competition for a job in a top business school, you could be looking at $120,000 for nine months, which would be $150,000 for 12 months not counting other choice opportunities; not too shabby for an academic job.

Base salaries for industry or consulting are unlikely to match the top business schools, but jobs in the private sector often offer bonuses, incentives, opportunities for rapid advancement, and a much higher maximum cap on salaries. Public sector salaries tend to run lower and have a much lower maximum salary.

*****

Adopting a popular song lyric, the future for I-O Psychology is so bright, you have to wear shades. However, predicting the future is always difficult when it comes to economic markets, and this is especially true of professional job markets, so we would not suggest that you go into I-O Psychology for the money. Obtaining an advanced degree is difficult if your heart is not in it. You should consider a career in I-O Psychology if you enjoy working with and serving people, studying the behavior of others, and applying your knowledge and experience in a real-world setting – the world of work and organizations. As you can see, there is a wide variety of work you can do, and if I-O interests you, we are confident you can have a rewarding and enjoyable career in the field.

PART 2

THE UNDERGRADUATE STUDENT YEARS

CHAPTER 3

Pursuing I-O Psychology as an Undergraduate

If you are currently working on your undergraduate degree and considering a career in I-O Psychology, or wondering what you could be doing to prepare yourself for such a career, you have come to the right place. Many colleagues of ours had not even heard of I-O Psychology until much later on, so consider yourself ahead of the curve. That said, there is still a great deal that can be done at this point to explore whether this field is right for you, prepare yourself for graduate study, and start assembling the building blocks of a competitive application for graduate schools.

We will cover the basics in this chapter and then, in Chapters 4 through 6, we will get into applying for and making decisions regarding graduate school. This chapter will delve into issues such as:

- What courses should I take?
- How to I prepare for graduate-level work?
- Should I do research?
- Should I try to get some work experience in a related area?

Two different perspectives on life as an undergraduate are offered. In Table 3.1, Kate Ferguson, a traditional undergraduate psychology student shares how she came to be interested in I-O and what she is doing to prepare for graduate school. Then, in Table 3.2, Cheryl Hardy describes her adventures as a more mature adult returning to college to pursue a psychology degree.

Table 3.1 Kate Ferguson, Undergraduate Psychology Student

Since high school, I always was interested in the sciences. I began my college career studying biology, with an interest in the medical field. I wanted my future career to help people. As I furthered my studies, I became interested in the psychology field. After switching my major to psychology, I realized I was at a loss as to what part of the field I found most interesting. This was when I learned more about I-O Psychology, which helped me figure things out. The first thing that interested me was the scientific approach. I-O Psychology uses the scientific method and applies it to common real-world experiences, like working in an office. The second part of I-O Psychology that caught my attention was the variety of career paths this field provided. Choosing to go to graduate school for I-O can lead me to various jobs, instead of only giving me one option like other graduate degrees. Thirdly, I feel that I can make a positive impact on people's lives through I-O Psychology. The main goal of an I-O psychologist is to improve the organizations' experience for its members and clientele.

I am fortunate enough to be able to seek I-O Psychology experiences as an undergraduate student in several ways. Not only am able to take an undergraduate class that focuses on I-O Psychology, I have also interned at the Center for Organizational Research (COR) at The University of Akron. This internship has greatly benefitted me in preparing for a graduate school program. Hands-on learning and observing in this setting gives me a deeper experience than just a textbook and gets me excited for my future career. While starting my work with COR, I created three goals for myself. The first was to familiarize myself with I-O terminology frequently used in consulting settings. This goal was to help me develop as a professional. Being able to use these terms with professionals, instead of just learning them in a classroom setting has helped prepare me for graduate school. My second goal was to gain a more complete understanding of the services provided by consulting firms like COR. The final goal I set for my internship was to acquire an understanding of how consulting firms carry out and complete these services for their clients. Fortunately, I have been able to accomplish and make great progress towards my goals.

As I continue my undergraduate journey, I plan on completing research, especially focusing on the organizational side. Gaining a wide variety of undergraduate experiences in this field will help me to determine future factors, such as whether I want to pursue a master's or doctoral degree after I graduate, and what type of future work I would be most interested in. Anyone who is interested in also pursuing these future endeavors should consider gaining hands-on experience as an undergraduate. This will not only help build résumés, but also help in deciding what types of post-undergraduate programs they are interested in pursuing.

Table 3.2 Cheryl Hardy, a Non-Traditional Student Pursuing I-O as an Undergraduate

When I returned to my undergraduate studies as an adult, I was unsure what I wanted to study. Nothing seemed to be a perfect fit for my interests. I talked with my professors about my interests in hopes that they would be able to direct me to a career that I had not previously considered. It was the professor of my management class who first introduced me to the term "I-O Psychology." The professor described it as "psychological principles applied to the workplace." This intrigued me, because I was interested in the subject of psychology, but I knew a career in counseling would not be a good fit for me, and I was unsure of other available options. I decided to learn more about workplace psychology.

The following semester, I took an I-O Psychology course where I learned the basics of the field. I learned that I-O Psychology is driven mainly by statistics, and that all aspects of the corporate world can be tested, analyzed, and the results applied to improve outcomes for a company. The information I learned regarding the hiring process intrigued me the most. For instance, the workplace problems often faced by I-O Psychologists can to some degree be prevented through good hiring practices. I realized that I was most interested in helping good companies find the right talent and helping good talent find the right company. A good employer-employee fit can often be determined through pre-employment testing and statistical analysis of that testing. When this happens, not only does employee satisfaction and productivity increase, but the company's atmosphere and bottom line also benefit.

Once I determined that I-O Psychology might be the perfect fit I was searching for, I sought out an internship which would expose me to the day-to-day work of those in the field. Fortunately, my university is home to an I-O Psychology consulting firm with which I was able to partner. In my time there, I was exposed to other aspects of the career including statistical analysis of a variety of measures, organizational development, job analysis, training, and developing customized tests and measures for various competencies.

As I prepare to apply for graduate school, I desire to take advantage of every opportunity available to me during my time as an undergrad. Upon completion of my internship, I intend to remain in contact with my supervisors to offer my continued assistance during periods of increased workload. I will also seek to expand my network by reaching out to other university professors and leaders in the field who could assist me in broadening my knowledge base and experience. I truly believe that going above and beyond the expectations of others is what will set me apart from other applicants and help me to achieve my scholarly, professional, and personal goals.

COURSEWORK

Our advice for what courses should be taken needs to be qualified by the course offerings available to you. If you are a Psychology major, you should already be on track to take a range of courses across different areas of specialization. General courses that will be very helpful in preparing you for graduate study include Social Psychology, Research Methods, and, especially, Tests and Measures.

Look into whether there are I-O Psychology courses offered, or whether any faculty at your institution has a degree in I-O Psychology or Organizational Behavior, either in the Psychology Department or a Business/Management Department. At some larger schools you will even find I-O faculty in the Industrial and Labor Relations Department. If there are I-O faculty at your institution, or even an I-O graduate program, you should take advantage of this opportunity by taking as many relevant courses as you can and starting to build connections with I-O professionals. This could involve an introductory course in I-O Psychology, or more advanced courses on topics such as diversity in the workplace, small groups and teams, stress and well-being at work, or leadership.

It may be that your institution does not offer any I-O courses through the Psychology Department. In that unfortunate case, you might want to consider checking out offerings through the Business College including courses with titles such as Introduction to Business, Management, Human Resource Management, and Organizational Behavior.

The earlier you familiarize yourself with statistics, the better. Taking a course on Statistics in the Social Sciences will be extremely helpful in understanding the research foundations of I-O Psychology; the exact title of the course can vary, alternative names for courses would include Quantitative Methods, Research Methods, and Experimental Psychology. If you end up enjoying your quantitative courses, adding a minor or just taking some advanced statistical modeling courses will give you a leg up. Becoming familiar with statistical packages is a huge plus; the more adept you are at *SPSS* the better, or familiarizing yourself with the hot new statistical package, *R*, would be a sure benefit.

Of course, not all institutions can provide the exact courses you would like to take to prepare yourself for graduate study in I-O. If this is the case, it might be worthwhile enrolling in an online course to explore whether this is something you are truly interested in pursuing.

READIN', 'RITIN', AND 'RITHMETIC

Beyond psychology, having a solid liberal arts background is a definite plus both in preparing for the Graduate Record Examination (GRE) and developing the skills you will need in graduate school. The biggest challenge most students encounter in graduate school is adjusting to the quantity and difficulty of the reading assignments. It is not unusual to have to read a couple of hundred pages of dense, difficult journal articles for each individual class.

Try to prepare for the reading load and increase your reading speed as an undergraduate. A recommended training method is taking English or Philosophy courses beyond the basic introductory requirements. Find a course where you have to read a novel a week, peruse volumes of poetry, or digest writings on existential philosophical thought. Train yourself to read quickly with comprehension. Increasing your reading ability will pay handsome dividends both on the GRE and in graduate school.

A similar comment applies to writing skills. Today, many new graduate students can construct amazing PowerPoint presentations, but struggle to write a coherent essay. As an undergraduate, look for classes with a heavy writing requirement. Work on and practice your rhetorical skills. If your knowledge of grammar is weak, or even if you are just looking for a light read that can refresh some principles, we recommend the classic book by Strunk and White (2000), *The Elements of Style*. Work on your word processing skills as well, the more proficient you become in Microsoft Word, the more valuable you will be as a research assistant to your future graduate school professors.

If you can, find and sign up for relevant math course. Even a basic class in calculus will make it easier to understand statistics; as will taking a statistics or statistical theory course through the math department. Given R appears to be the future go-to program, consider taking a course in R, or other relevant computer science courses in coding or big data analytics.

RESEARCH OR FIELD EXPERIENCE

Gaining experience in fieldwork through an internship would certainly be valuable, but we would argue that undergraduates should focus more on participating in research. Research experience is extremely important if you are planning to apply to a graduate school in any field of psychology, both in the sense that it will strengthen your application, and in that it will give you a realistic preview of what your life in graduate school will entail.

Our advice would be to start identifying possible research opportunities as early as possible in your undergraduate career.

If you do not know where to get started with becoming involved in research, find out whether a psychology professor whose class you enjoyed has an active research lab and is open to taking on a new research assistant. Do not be afraid to talk to faculty and graduate students. They are there to help you. Ideally, you will find a good match where the lab is active in a certain area of research that you find interesting. Look into several opportunities so that you can decide what would be the best fit based on the opportunities and time you can dedicate to lab work.

TEXTBOX 3.1 GET TO KNOW YOUR FACULTY

A challenge: If you are an undergraduate student, how many of the faculty at your university can you name? How many would be able to write a letter of reference for you? Most people become faculty because they like working with students, so do not be afraid to go see them during office hours and introduce yourself. Not only will you need faculty members to write letters of reference for you, but they are also a great source of information on courses you should take, preparing for the GRE, and the types of graduate programs which would be the best fit given your grades and interests. Consider joining Psychology Club or Psi Chi as two other avenues to meeting graduate students and faculty.

Working in an I-O lab can help you to focus in on your future research interests. Even if you find an opening in a lab within a different subfield of Psychology, you can learn valuable skills that will transfer regardless of the specific research topic.

Tasks for research assistants can vary a great deal. You may be running experiments, entering data, or recruiting participants, which will all help you gain an understanding of the research process. You may be working directly with faculty members, graduate students, or both, which can give you an opportunity to observe and learn advanced research skills such as data analysis and designing experiments. As you gain more experience in your role, you may be given additional independent work, such as conducting a literature review to help in designing a new study.

Aside from working as a research assistant, there may be opportunities to gain experience in the form of a senior thesis, honors project, or other independent research project. This will typically start with identifying a faculty advisor or mentor, reading published research papers within their area of expertise, and then designing and carrying out a research study that can address a problem or clarify a process within that topic area. Going through this experience with guidance from your advisor will go a long way in preparing for the next tier of research, such as a master's thesis.

Who knows, maybe you will even get the paper published in a journal. Not only will a published paper as an undergraduate student make your family and friends proud, it will also look very impressive on your résumé when applying for graduate school. Remember, professors in graduate programs are evaluated and rewarded based on their research, so seeing an applicant with published research is like finding the pot of gold at the end of the rainbow.

Field experience is another option, although less likely to assist you in getting into graduate school. Obtaining a job in human resources can provide you with an insider's look at the field. If you do have a job, talk to a professor as to whether it would be possible to do some type of field project at work. Most organizations would be receptive, and your professor should be happy to have a chance to make contacts in a local organization.

HONOR SOCIETIES

Most colleges have several honorary societies and clubs that offer opportunities to engage in leadership and service. Although membership to any organization will be a positive on a graduate application, you should consider applying for organizations related to psychology. Check and see if your department has a Psychology Club; which is a great way to meet other students and faculty. Then, when you are ready, apply for membership in Psi Chi, which is a psychology honorary society. Not only will such experiences improve your graduate application, participation in extracurricular activities is often prized by industry when they are hiring for job openings. Plus, such societies provide a starting point in developing a network of future professional contacts.

*****

College should be fun, but from day one you should also be aiming for a goal. Admission to graduate school is highly competitive, so we recommend you take as many I-O–related courses as you can, and work hard on keeping those grades up. If you dream of attending graduate school, focus on activities that build your case and will make you an attractive applicant in the eyes of graduate programs. Mainly this should take the form of dedication to studies, which should translate into high levels of performance in challenging classes, and also involvement in other activities like research and honor societies.

Chapter 4

Applying to Graduate School

Chapter 3 discussed how to prepare as an undergraduate for those anxiety-inducing days when you apply to graduate school. Chapter 5 will cover the different types of graduate programs, and Chapter 6 deals with what to do when you are faced with the difficult choice between competing offers. In this chapter, the focus is on applying for graduate school. Specifically, we will delve into issues such as:

- What do I need to do to create an effective application to graduate school?
- How do I write my personal statement?
- The Graduate Record Examination or GRE.
- Who should I ask for letters of recommendation?

Managing the process of applying to graduate school can be tricky for any student, however, it is even more challenging for the international student seeking to study in the U.S. In Table 4.1, Ketaki Sodhi discusses the challenges she encountered as an undergraduate in India and how she dealt with the various obstacles.

APPLYING TO GRADUATE SCHOOL

Once your decision to apply to graduate school has been made, you should start creating a plan and timeline to make the process as stress-free as possible. Application deadlines for U.S. graduate programs in I-O Psychology range from October to February, although most occur between early December and mid-January. Each year the deadlines seem to keep getting earlier and earlier, so be prepared.

Table 4.1 Ketaki Sodhi, M.A., India to Akron: How an International Student Landed at The University of Akron

When I entered college, my goal was to major in developmental economics. In my freshman year, I was assigned a class project which required me to study and write a paper on someone who has received a Nobel Prize in economics, and I chose Daniel Kahneman. Kahneman, who I learned is actually a psychologist, won the Nobel Prize for his work on judgment and decision making.

After reading his book *Thinking Fast and Slow*, I started getting interested in psychology and took more classes related to psychology. After taking a class in I-O Psychology, I realized this was something I really enjoyed learning about and wanted to pursue it as a career. I got my undergraduate degree from the University of Mumbai, India but unfortunately India has very few good I-O Psychology graduate programs. Given this, I had expanded my search to graduate schools in the U.S.

As an international student, there were a few challenges I faced. Firstly, knowing which schools would be a good fit for me was hard since I only had access to online resources. Luckily, SIOP has a comprehensive list of schools along with key features of each school. In addition to this, SIOP also publishes rankings of top I-O programs based on different criteria (such as program culture and publications). Using these resources along with faculty research interests, I determined which schools would be the best fit and applied to roughly six schools.

A second challenge during this process was figuring out how my degree and experiences in undergrad mapped on to those in the U.S. educational system. For this I sought the advice of USIEF (United States-India Educational Foundation), which is an international foundation dedicated to higher education in India and the United States. They guided me through the process and helped me better understand the U.S. education system.

A third big concern for me was not being able to visit schools and meet with faculty members or potential advisors because of my location. As a substitute, I emailed the faculty I was interested in working with and set up Skype calls to discuss research as well as other school-related concerns with them. In addition to this, I reached out to schools that invited me for their visit day to get a sense of what the program culture and realities of being a grad student are like.

Finally, my biggest challenge was deciding which school to attend after receiving offers. Using a combination of all the resources and conversations mentioned above as well as after talking with alumni from each school and weighing potential for future prospects, I chose to attend the Ph.D. program at The University of Akron. Thankfully I am very happy with my choice of school.

I believe that talking to multiple different people such as faculty, students, and alumni as well as using factual information such as the SIOP resources and department websites helped me get a complete sense of the different programs. I currently work in the ACTION lab studying interpersonal dynamics in teamwork and collaboration. In addition to this, I serve as a director for COR (Center for Organizational Research), which is the in-house consulting center at The University of Akron. I wish to pursue a career in applied research and I think my experiences in grad school will set me really well to make that a reality.

On an ideal timeline, you would start the process ten months ahead of time, or in March of your Junior year. As a note, this timeline assumes that you are applying to graduate school in your senior year of a traditional four-year program. We take this perspective because we see this as the most common approach among students considering graduate school, but we acknowledge that there are many possible paths, and a fair number of applicants choose to work full-time for a period after graduation before applying to graduate school. Ultimately, there is no one-size-fits-all solution and you will have to determine the best path for you based on your individual situation. That said, we have provided a sample timeline in Table 4.2.

The first major step is researching programs to compile an initial list of schools. You should decide what type of program you are applying to (e. g., master's or Ph.D., traditional or online; we cover types of programs in the next chapter), and then start looking into specific programs based on the information you can gather online (the SIOP website is a great place to start) and by reaching out to current students. Information that will be needed will include:

- Admission requirements, including minimum and typical GRE and GPA.
- Quality of the program or ranking.
- Location.
- Names of program faculty.
- Research, theoretical, and practical interests of program faculty.
- Graduate assistantships and funding.
- Costs.
- Program culture.

Table 4.2 Ideal Timeline for Pursuing I-O Psychology as a Traditional
Undergraduate

Freshman Year

- Declare a psychology major.
- Take foundational psychology courses (e.g., Introduction to Psychology).
- Visit professors at office hours and discuss your interest in I-O Psychology.

Sophomore Year

- Continue taking foundational psychology courses.
- Consider joining Psychology Club and applying for membership in Psi Chi (if there is a branch at your institution).
- Visit professors at office hours or schedule a meeting with an I-O Psychology professor.
- Look into different research labs and learn about their current projects.
- Find out about the process for joining a research lab; apply for a research assistant position if open.
- Think about what program type would be good for you based on your research interests and career goals.

Junior Year

- Take advanced psychology courses (i.e., Research Methods).
- Join a research lab if you have not; look into other labs that may supplement your experience.
- Decide on program type and start to identify a preliminary list of specific programs, faculty, and research areas.
- Consider who you could ask for a letter of recommendation and work to fill in any gaps.
- Start thinking about an outline for your personal statement.
- Create a timeline for studying for the GRE and choose a test date.

Summer after Junior Year

- Prepare for and take the GRE.
- Finalize list of graduate programs you will apply to.
- Compile application requirements for your list of programs in a way that is convenient.
- Write your personal statement.
- Create or update your résumé and send it to someone for feedback.

Senior Year
Before application deadlines (October through February of Senior Year)

- Continue taking advanced psychology courses.
- Continue work in research lab or labs. If possible, work on an independent project related to your research interests.

- Send your personal statement draft to several people for feedback.
- Finalize personal statements per the requirements for each program.
- Ask for letters of recommendation and follow up.
- Request transcripts from your University.
- Compile application materials and submit applications.
- Check with school to make sure all materials have been received and nothing is missing.

After application deadlines (January through March of Senior Year)

- Consider applying for financial aid for graduate school; fill out Free Application for Federal Student Aid, or FAFSA.
- Relax and wait to hear from programs!
- Once you hear from programs, start process of a detailed evaluation of all offers (See Chapter 6).
- If invited, visit potential programs to meet faculty and get a realistic view and sense of fit.
- Talk with current students about their experience in the programs you are considering.
- Give your acceptance as soon as your final decision has been made.
- National Acceptance Deadline: April 15th.

TEXTBOX 4.1 THE EMAIL REQUESTING A GRADUATE POSITION IN THE LAB

Some resources suggest you reach out to professors in a graduate programs to ask them if they will consider you for a position in your lab. Whether that email has any chance of being effective depends on the type of program. Some schools are more program-centric, the faculty as a whole consider and accept students, in which case a personal communication of this type will have only a small chance of increasing your probability of admittance. Other schools may be more faculty-centric, in which case individual faculty do consider and admit students, although we are still unsure how much an individual email helps given the number received by many professors. If you are going to send an email, then try to make it accurate, convincing, and well-written. That means you should spell the faculty member's name correctly, list the right area of research, and try to make it seem like you did not send the same exact email to 100 other faculty members.

Most schools require a fee when you apply, which can run from free to 50 dollars. So, you will need a budget and funds set aside for applying to graduate schools. Applying for ten programs, including application fees, transcript fees, and fees for sending GRE scores, could run you around $500, not counting all of your lost time.

Visiting programs will require additional funds. If this is starting to worry you, know that there are options available to ease this burden. You should investigate scholarships, fellowships, and grants that might be offered within your undergraduate institution for professional development. Of course, another option is to take out loans, although student debt is rising to astronomical levels, and we would exert caution in recommending that option.

Once you have chosen the schools you will apply to, you can work on organizing all the application materials. A simple spreadsheet with all the necessary information will be helpful in keeping track of everything from materials and deadlines to online portal logins and passwords. Different schools will have distinct requirements for submitting transcripts, different prompts or word limits for the personal statement, and additional supplemental requirements, so it is important to be thorough and detail-oriented. We wish that psychology could modernize this process as some other professions have done; however, the current reality is that you will probably have to repeat the same information on application after application, with appropriate individualization of the information.

Studying for and taking the GRE should be your next major focus, followed by writing and revising your personal statement, and asking for letters of recommendation. We discuss each of these in further detail in the following sections.

GRE® GENERAL TEST

The GRE General Test is a standardized test that most graduate programs in I-O Psychology require as part of the application package. These scores are helpful in that they give admissions committees a common metric to use in comparing applicants. The test has three main sections and results are reported in three scores: Verbal Reasoning, Quantitative Reasoning, and Analytical Writing. The scores are scaled from 130 to 170 for both the Verbal and Quantitative portions, and 0 to 6 for the Writing portion. The test is delivered in testing centers, and most commonly in a computer-based format.

When you identify the specific programs that you are interested in, many will list average or minimum GRE scores on their admissions websites. These standards can give you an idea of where your target score should be, or whether you would be a good match for a program once you have taken the test. Generally speaking, graduate admissions committees will focus more heavily on the Verbal and Quantitative scores, and scores above 160, which equates to the 83rd percentile and would make you competitive for even the best Ph.D. programs. A score of 155 would be above many school's minimums and, depending on your GPA, give you a fighting chance of being selected by most programs. A score at 150 or below would make it difficult to get into the top Ph.D. programs, unless you have other unique characteristics as an applicant.

You can sign up for the test and reserve a spot on the GRE website. There is a fee to take the test, but you can access plenty of study materials for free online. Application deadlines range from around October to February, so, if you were to dedicate the summer to test preparation and take the test in July or August, you should be in good shape from a timeline perspective.

You should plan to take the GRE as early as possible so that you can focus on the other parts of your application, or, if you do poorly on the GRE, retake the test with enough time to replace the scores. If you do have a low GRE score, then you will want to apply to more master's programs. You can use your performance in a master's program to demonstrate your ability to do graduate school work to Ph.D. programs in the future.

Most schools use some type of algorithm or formula to add together the GPA and GRE to arrive at a single score. Thus, there is a tradeoff between GRE and your GPA. Although you want to keep both above the minimum and also as high as possible, a slightly lower GPA can be compensated for by outstanding GRE scores, and vice versa.

Additionally, some programs require the GRE Psychology subject test, which is a more specialized test that covers knowledge within the most common subfields of psychology such as social, cognitive, and developmental areas. As a final note, if you are applying to schools in a different country, there may be additional testing required.

PERSONAL STATEMENT

Ultimately the more objective measures, such as your GPA and GRE scores, will hold more weight, but a compelling personal statement can be a deciding factor between two applications that look similar on those other characteristics. Your personal statement is your opportunity to sell yourself to the graduate faculty and convince them that you will make an outstanding contribution as a student. This as an opportunity to explain any weak areas in your application. For instance, if you have never taken an I-O Psychology course, you should make sure to emphasize what exactly interests you within I-O and what you have done in other ways to gain an understanding of psychology in the workplace.

As a general template, you could start with an introduction that describes your career goals and why you are interested in I-O Psychology, whether it is a story about a work-related problem you encountered, or a construct that you found compelling in class. The body of your statement can describe a few key developmental experiences that show you are prepared for graduate-level study. Here, you can discuss your role in a lab, for example, from your perspective and in greater detail than in a résumé, expanding on what you see as the main takeaways from that experience. If there are factors that explain a poor semester in college, such as an illness, this is your chance to explain why your grades for a certain period in your life are not representative. As a conclusion, you should describe your more immediate goals and how you think you would fit into the program to which you are applying.

Before beginning to write a personal statement, we suggest you think deeply about questions like: *Why do I want this? Why do I want this now? Where do I see myself in a future career? What have I done to build the skills to get there?* These big-picture questions can help you get started. When you have a completed draft, send it to several people who can provide constructive feedback.

Finally, you will want to tailor your personal statement to each graduate program for which you are applying. *Are there particular faculty you would like to work with? Do faculty have an area of research where you believe you would offer a good fit? Would you offer a diverse perspective? Why are you a good fit to the overall program? Have you worked with faculty in your undergraduate program who recommended you consider a specific program?*

One common mistake is to make yourself look like you are really trying to get into a clinical or counseling program but applying to an I-O option as a matter of convenience. Make sure you letter explains why you find I-O to be an attractive option. Another common mistake is trying to tailor your letter but misspelling faculty names or incorrectly identifying their major research areas. Be careful and detail-oriented when constructing your letters. As a guide, a Personal Statement Checklist appears in Table 4.3.

If you are an international or foreign student, the program may request that you also provide information on how you intend to cover the costs associated with graduate study. International students should make the program aware of any potential barriers to attending school in the United States, and should clearly state that all such problems or conflicts can be overcome.

Table 4.3 Personal Statement Checklist

Background

- Why are you pursuing I-O Psychology?
- What are your research interests or areas in which you wish to specialize?
- Explain any weak points or potential concerns.

Experience

- What have you done to this point to prepare you for a graduate level education?
- Focus in and elaborate on one or two developmental experiences which allowed you to work on certain skills or raise awareness of some issue.

Goals

- What are your career goals (i.e., applied, academic, unsure and want to gain experience in both areas)?
- Why are you applying to the specific program; why do you think it will be a good fit?
- Which faculty members (1–2) are you interested in working with and why?

LETTERS OF RECOMMENDATION

Graduate school applications will typically require three or four letters of recommendation, and it is never too early to start thinking of who could be a potential recommender for you. The best letter will come from somebody who can speak to your academic ability, your work ethic, and your interest in attending graduate school in I-O. A professor whose class you received an A in your freshman year, but never spoke with outside of class would probably not know you well enough to write a compelling letter. You can avoid such a letter by keeping this in mind early on, visiting professors at their office hours, taking an interest in their research, and asking for their advice about your career goals.

A good choice would be a psychology faculty member who has supervised your work in a research lab or independent study, as they would be able to speak to your competencies and preparation for graduate study outside of the classroom. However, sometimes work in a research lab is structured in a way that there is not a lot of contact with the principal faculty member, and instead you work more closely with graduate students. In these cases, psychology graduate students, especially I-O Psychology graduate students would be able to provide a strong letter of recommendation as well. Next, you should consider asking faculty or graduate student instructors of psychology or business courses that you excelled in, and as mentioned this person should know you outside of class as well. Finally, a supervisor at a job or internship could be used as a recommender, especially if you are taking some time to work after completing your undergraduate degree. This is not always possible, but it is worth mentioning that graduate programs are probably most impressed if one of your letter writers is an alumnus of their own program, as Ph.D. programs are naturally proud of graduates who have gone on to academic jobs.

An important point to mention is to make sure to be as considerate as possible throughout the process, as your letter writers will be spending their time to try to help you in your goals. We recommend that our undergraduate students create a portfolio to give to each person that has agreed to write a letter. This should contain your transcript, personal statement, résumé, and a sample of an academic paper you have written. This will allow your writers to speak to different areas and create a well-rounded description of your qualifications.

You should also include a list of the schools you are applying to, the due dates for the letters, and the platform for submission for each school (online or via mail). If some letters need to be sent in the mail, you can pre-address and stamp envelopes to make it as easy as possible for them, although in some cases this may be a task handled by the departmental secretaries, so check with a faculty member first.

*****

Applying to graduate school will require time, effort, money, and most of all, effective organization. The earlier you start the better, which for a traditional student, means beginning the process of applying to graduate programs in your junior year of college. We outline the process as starting with finding your list of programs, and then solidifying competitive GRE scores, writing a compelling personal statement, and soliciting your letters of recommendation. However, as discussed in Chapter 3, you should be working to set yourself up in certain areas well before that (e.g., maintaining a high GPA, gaining research experience). In the next chapter, we will discuss the many options to consider in terms of types of graduate school programs.

Chapter 5

Types of I-O Graduate Programs

There are a myriad of different types of I-O programs, each of which has unique attributes and vary in the type of educational experiences that are offered. You should know a little bit about the options for graduate study so that you can determine what general type of program is best suited to your career goals. Once you have an idea of program type, you can further narrow this down to a specific graduate program, which can vary in faculty specialty areas, research or applied emphasis, and whether they encourage or require internships. In this chapter, we provide a brief review of:

- I-O master's programs
- I-O Ph.D. programs
- I-O Psy.D. programs
- Business programs
- Online versus traditional I-O programs

If you would like information on the different types of programs, a great place to go is the SIOP website. There you will find a whole tab or section for students. This includes a link to program rankings based on different criteria, which you may find very helpful.

In this chapter, a career vignette is included in Table 5.1 from Eric Hutchison. His career follows a nontraditional route, where he found the best match for his life demands was an online program. In addition, while pursuing a Ph.D., Eric works in the public sector and also teaches classes.

Table 5.1 Eric S. Hutchison, M.B.A., M.S., Transitioning and Pursuing I-O in an Online Program

My desire to earn a Ph.D. started in 2003. As a working student in an M.B.A. program, my employer was involved in a large merger initiative, and I was fascinated by the organizational behavior component, as well as the way change was being managed. However, embarking on this adventure took several years of planning because of the commitment and resources that would be required to start another academic program. During the planning phase, I changed companies twice. Many of the experiences during this time contributed to identifying the reason why I wanted to earn a Ph.D. My goal in getting a Ph.D. is to make a difference in the way companies hire, develop, and engage employees, and I believe I can contribute to these areas through teaching, consulting, and researching. Through this identification process, I decided to study I-O Psychology.

After extensive exploration of traditional and nontraditional programs, which included discussions with mentors in academia, I decided on an online program at Walden University. The primary decision factor was the flexibility I needed because of my family and work obligations. Second, I was at a point in my career where I wanted to make a change. Although the nontraditional program has required participation through asynchronous communication and due dates for assignments, this platform also provided an opportunity to participate and complete projects without having to be online or in a classroom at specific times.

I have more than 20 years of professional experience and 13 years of teaching at the college level. Although I had held leadership positions, my background was not in I-O Psychology. I perceived this as a challenge, but this was not a problem with Walden. The experience I have with corporations and education provided an opportunity to engage with C-level clients, participate in request for proposal processes, conduct financial analysis, and engage in strategic planning. The I-O degree strengthens these skills and adds the selection, development, diagnosis, and research components. Also, the scholar-practitioner approach at Walden included approaching real-world challenges through course material and assignments with a strong focus on social change.

I am currently teaching at three different colleges and have a consulting business with a focus on strategic planning and organizational development. I work with the Civil Service Commission in Columbus, Ohio, which is responsible for designing and implementing the assessment and selection process for first responders. I am engaged on the board of trustees for the Huckleberry House, a nonprofit youth crisis organization, volunteer for Meals on Wheels, and am on the Membership and Club Capacity Committees for the Athletic Club of Columbus.

I share these current work experiences because they are very different from the career I had before starting the doctorate program. Although I leverage my previous experience on a regular basis, the work I am doing today is different because of my experience in Walden's I-O program. The difference I can make with assessment, selection, development, and strategic planning is more significant because of the skills I developed through the coursework phase of the doctoral program. I will begin my dissertation this month and will be focusing on the effect of community involvement in the assessment and selection of police officers. The results of this study can provide insights into the effect of evaluation methods on selection outcomes and the validity of an entry-level police officer selection assessment. These findings could aid local Civil Service Commissions and other entry-level police officer selection committees identify the best approach for providing equal access to jobs while predicting the performance of applicants.

TEXTBOX 5.1 A MASTER'S OR A PH.D. DEGREE?

We often see prospective applicants grapple with is whether to go for a master's or Ph.D. program. Unfortunately, we cannot resolve that issue here, as there are many pros and cons to both. Instead, in this chapter, we outline the most important considerations so as to help you make the best decision.

MASTER'S OF ARTS (M.A.) OR MASTER'S OF SCIENCE (M.S.)

Master's programs require about two years of full-time study. The goal of I-O master's programs is to provide students with a broad knowledge base of I-O Psychology and prepare them for a career as an I-O professional. There is more of an emphasis on practical skills and on applying I-O theories in the real world in a master's program, compared with doctoral programs. Programs may require an applied internship to help students further develop those skills.

Despite the applied focus, some programs may still require the completion of a master's thesis and work in a research lab. A master's thesis is an independent research project that can contribute to the I-O research literature. Even if your goals are not related to conducting research in an academic setting, it is fundamental in the field of I-O, which strongly emphasizes evidence-based practice. A master's degree in I-O would prepare you for a wide variety of jobs in industry, which could be internal roles such as an HR generalist in an organization, or external roles such as a junior consultant at a firm specializing in selection tools.

Applying to master's programs can still be competitive, but standards for GPA and GRE scores are lower than those for Ph.D. programs. Those weighing the options of pursuing a master's or a Ph.D. should consider benefits such as less schooling time for the master's and getting out into the workforce more quickly, and thus making money more rapidly. On the other hand, tuition costs can add up quickly, while traditional Ph.D. programs usually come with a tuition waiver. You can refer to salary studies done by SIOP, which illustrate the sizable salary difference, with those with master's degrees having lower starting salaries compared with Ph.D. graduates.

DOCTOR OF PHILOSOPHY (PH.D.)

Ph.D. programs require a significantly longer investment, typically five or six years as a full-time student. Many programs are structured so that students obtain a master's degree in the first two or three years, and then continue toward the Ph.D. by completing additional coursework and a doctoral dissertation. Some Ph.D. programs will admit students who already have completed a master's degree elsewhere, while other programs prefer applicants with a bachelor's degree. Those who are interested in teaching or academia would need the Ph.D., while those interested in an applied career have more of a choice between the master's and doctorate.

The goal of I-O doctoral programs is to train students to become I-O scholars and contributors to the field, so there is an expectation to be more involved in research throughout your program, regardless of whether you want a career in academia or research. Programs vary widely in the degree to which they emphasize and balance teaching, research, and applied experience for their graduate students, so you should seek to find a match with the experiences you desire in graduate school.

Doctoral program admissions tend to be more competitive than master's programs and this results in higher admission standards including research experience, higher GPAs as undergraduates, and higher GRE scores. Part of the reason for this added competition is because most doctoral programs offer tuition waivers during your time as a student, greatly reducing the cost of the education. They also typically offer a graduate assistantship, which can cover some living expenses and allows you to complete part-time work within the department, usually either as a teaching or research assistant. There is greater flexibility in the type of job you can attain after graduate school with a Ph.D., whether your primary interest lies in academia, consulting, the public sector, or industry.

MASTER'S OR PH.D.?

The most common question we see is whether to go for a master's or Ph. D. in I-O Psychology. This best decision for you will depend on how you weigh the different aspects we touched on, there are plenty of pros and cons to both and there is no right answer. You should think about things like: *Do I want an applied career, or one in academia? Am I eager to get into the workforce quickly, or am I willing to invest in a longer degree path? Do I have the financial resources to get a degree on my own, or do I need a fully funded program to make it happen? Am I restricted because of family and, therefore, need the convenience of an online program?*

DOCTOR OF PSYCHOLOGY (PSY.D.)

Psy.D. programs, also referred to as "Professional Psychology" programs or "Sci Ds," also lead to a doctorate, but typically have a greater emphasis on the applied side, including field experiences and internships, and less of an emphasis on research. The dissertation, which serves as a significant roadblock to many in obtaining a Ph.D., may be replaced with some type of capstone project or paper, or at least be modified to reduce the requirement for a lengthy, original research study. Due to this emphasis, many Psy.D. programs can be completed in four years.

The shorter time to finish means you can be out earning a salary much faster. The downside is that Psy.D. programs are less likely to offer graduate assistantships and so you may graduate with significantly more debt. Of course, if you have acquired a good job with a high salary, you may be able to pay off your loans while your peers in Ph.D. programs are still trying to finish their dissertation.

BUSINESS SCHOOL

The field of management is very closely related to I-O, with many I-O graduates going on to teach at business schools in Management or Organizational Behavior departments. Getting a Ph.D. in one of these programs might be for you if you are certain that you want a career in academia. Some business schools also offer the Doctorate in Business Administration, or D.B.A.

A master's in Business Administration (M.B.A.) is another option to consider. This degree is practice-oriented and covers evidence-based approaches to management in a broad sense, including various areas such as accounting, business law, and marketing, though specializations in one area are common. M.B.A. programs have a variety of options providing flexibility for those interested in full-time, part-time, accelerated, weekend, or online study. Because of the much broader breadth of knowledge, we do not see many M.B.A.s in I-O practitioner roles. Instead, we have heard more of practitioners going back to get an M.B.A. after joining the workforce, especially those who want to supplement their I-O training with generalized business knowledge and acumen. An understanding of the financial side of your company through accounting and finance knowledge for example, is helpful in communicating I-O findings to diverse audiences. An M.B.A with a concentration in Human Resources or Organizational Behavior would also be an excellent choice if you have decided to seek generalist jobs as a human resource manager.

ONLINE PROGRAMS

Today, prospective applicants face a choice between what we have labeled "traditional" programs, those usually housed in a state, public, or private college or university with a physical building and location, sometime referred to as "brick-and-mortar," and online programs, also referred to as "distance" or "virtual" programs, where the student completes most of their coursework on a computer. Many online programs also offer weeks or weekends in residence, where the residence may be a physical location of the university or a hotel in a major city. There are also "blended" programs, which offer a mix of traditional and online classes, as well as research activities.

An increasing number of I-O professionals are coming out of online I-O programs. Currently, most of those programs offer master's degrees, but a few offer Ph.D.s as well. These programs tend to be targeted toward individuals who want to become practitioners as opposed to academics. In terms of the coursework, the content and learning should be the same for online versus traditional courses, if they are structured the same way. However, that is just one component of the graduate school. There are likely large differences in the entirety of the graduate school experience in an online program; some important aspects of a traditional program are very difficult to recreate in this setting. A traditional program offers more meaningful interaction with faculty and fellow graduate students, thus employers might expect graduate students in traditional programs to be more experienced in public speaking, presentation, and research. However, an online program does offer more experience with independent work and collaborating in a virtual setting.

There are some issues with the perception of online programs, but it is not clear if this is due to perceived quality of programs or the actual quality. That being said, there is likely to be a difference in perceptions of an online program from a reputable institution with I-O Ph.D. faculty, compared with a purely online university. If you are considering an online program, you can identify how comparable the quality is by whether the faculty have an I-O background, the amount and types of courses offered, whether a thesis is required, whether an internship is required, and whether there is a comprehensive exam.

TEXTBOX 5.2 DIFFICULTY FINDING INFORMATION ON ONLINE PROGRAMS?

Skeptics of online programs point to the fact that detailed program information like that on structure, requirements, and faculty background are often hard to find.

As an applicant, you should be realistic in recognizing that your career options may be limited if you go the online route. Ultimately, you need to consider your purpose and the competencies you will develop in that program. If you already work in HR and want the additional coursework to supplement your knowledge, an online program may be a better fit than if you want to attend a graduate program with the intention of pursuing an academic career.

*****

We hope this chapter has provided some clarity as to what program option might be best for you. If instead you are now more confused than before, we advise undergraduates who are undecided to identify and apply to several types of programs, which would allow you keep your options open. We want to emphasize once again that there are a lot of ways to become an I-O Psychologist and there is no right or wrong path with the type of program you pursue; by considering the different options you are already well-positioned to make the best decision based on your unique circumstances and goals. Hopefully, you receive multiple admission offers and at that point can make your final choice. In the next chapter, we deal with the very happy possibility that you do receive several acceptances from programs and then have to make your final decision.

CHAPTER 6

Decisions, Decisions, Decisions

Selecting the Right Program and Offer

Congratulations! At this point you have received several offers for admission into graduate school. You have celebrated with family, friends, and undergraduate faculty. Now comes the tough part, deciding which offer to accept. In this chapter, we offer advice on how to make the tough choice between the letters of acceptance you have received from different graduate programs. Making a final decision requires weighing several factors to arrive at the best decision given your unique situation and is a highly personal matter. This is the time to really think about what you want out of graduate school and which offer will help you best obtain your career goals, while still allowing you to balance your work, school, life, and family commitments. Some common factors to consider in exercising due diligence regarding this crucial life decision include:

- Timelines
- Monetary value of the offer
- Location
- Fit with faculty and other students
- Quality or ranking of the program
- Program type: Master's or Ph.D.

As this book was being written, Russell Steiner applied to I-O graduate programs, was admitted, and had to make an important choice. For those reasons, he shares his story of navigating the application and decision-making process in Table 6.1.

Table 6.1 Russell Steiner, A Journey in Applying to Graduate School

I have always had great respect for the academic achievements of my family: my mother was valedictorian of her high school, earned a medical degree, and leads her life as a top researcher in internal medicine. My father earned his Ph.D. in particle physics and went on to oversee online education at the American Museum of Natural History. My family background provided a foundation for my intellectual curiosity, which was something I always embraced and have been grateful for. While I was inherently passionate about academic learning, I have always had a greater love for people. I have been a natural social facilitator since I was in elementary school, where I would spend time communicating and coordinating among friends to create an epic playdate. I have always had an inherent fascination with people and being able to help them.

Initially, I took an interest in clinical psychology during high school. I felt I was someone many people turned to for help. I ended up enrolling in Advance Placement Psychology, and it still stands as one of the best, most influential classes I have taken to this day. During the summer after my senior year of high school, I realized that I did not want to confine myself to a traditional, clinical setting. Despite my interest in individual therapy, I wanted to practice psychology in a capacity that would satisfy my social drive. When a good friend told me about I-O Psychology and I read more about its focus, I knew this field would be right for me. Within I-O, I would be afforded a path towards combining my passions of learning about people and working together with many of them.

I entered Boston University with clear goals for getting to where I wanted to be. I enrolled in a dual-degree program in psychology and communication, thinking this combination would allow me to gain an understanding of management, while also preparing me for a job in human resources. I was involved in several labs and engaged in both natural and social scientific research, which fueled an excitement for recognizing patterns through empiricism and data interpretation. From the beginning, I planned to gain relevant work experience before continuing my I-O studies in a doctoral program. Upon graduation, after a few job prospects that did not seem like the right fit, I met the Chief Executive Officer of the company I now work for in a bar and explained my story to him. He appreciated my integrity and passion for people, and told me about the floral startup company, UrbanStems, that he had recently founded. Somehow, this chance encounter turned into a job offer.

It immediately seemed like the perfect opportunity. As the company's third hire, I was given the opportunity to play an integral role in growing a company from its inception. I had a clear vision then of the organizational experiences I would gain by laying the foundation for scaling a startup. I got to participate in, learn, and work with teams in all kinds of business areas like customer service, marketing, and finance. Two years in, I became our People Operations Manager and was tasked with creating, managing, and scaling our formal human resources department. We were about 70 staff members strong when I took on the endeavor and we have since doubled in size. I learned more about the processes involved in developing organizational infrastructures more than I ever thought possible three years out of college.

When I began managing our human resources department, I gave myself a goal of having one year of pure HR experience before applying to graduate school. Five months prior to taking the GRE, I began studying intensely, dedicating about four hours of preparation almost every evening after work. I then created a spreadsheet of graduate schools, which detailed deadlines, average GRE scores, program contacts, letters of recommendation, individual essay status; all the details necessary to ensure I was applying optimally. Getting into a doctoral program had been my goal and all of my work up to that point was to achieve it, so I was committed to investing as much of myself as possible those months. After hearing rejections, wait-lists, and acceptances, I was elated to get an offer from the program I have had my eyes on as the gold standard for I-O Psychology since I was an undergrad, The University of Akron. I will begin this summer of 2018 and continue my journey of becoming an I-O Psychologist.

PRACTICING DUE DILIGENCE

Deciding on a graduate program will dictate how you spend the next several years of your life, as well as the path of your eventual career. Thus, this is by no means a simple choice and there are a lot of factors to consider. Making your final decision requires extensive background research, much more than in the application stage, in order to compare your options and find the program that works best for you, provides the best fit, and has the highest overall utility. If you were unsure of what program types to apply for, and therefore applied to a wide range of possible schools, you may have offers from both master's and Ph.D. programs.

For master's offers, the applied experience offered through faculty members should be a major consideration. For Ph.D. offers, we think you should focus primarily on your fit with the research interests of potential faculty and advisors. Look into some of your prospective mentor's recent or current projects and see if those areas of research are of interest to you. In addition, if your dream is to someday be a consultant, the availability of internships and the business connections of the faculty should be considered.

Although less frequent than with Clinical and Counseling programs, some schools may require an in-person interview prior to acceptance or may offer a visit day around the time the initial offers have been sent out. You should make every effort to attend the visit days and see in person as many programs as you can. Although this will involve a substantial expense, there is nothing that can compare to physically visiting a campus and the surrounding city or town for a realistic preview of what the next few years of your life will be like. If you plan to make a trip to campus outside of a formal visit day, set up appointments with faculty and current graduate students ahead of time and come prepared with a list of questions you want and need answered.

You should also browse program websites and manuals to understand the structure of each program, course offerings, and opportunities for internships or teaching experiences. Sifting through all of this can be stressful and time-consuming but having a number of choices is a good problem to have, and taking the time to make a thoughtful decision will pay off in a smooth transition to graduate school.

TIMELINES

If you are requesting a graduate assistantship and applying to a traditional program, you will probably receive offers sometime in January, February, March, or April. We realize this is a pretty generous time window, but programs make their decisions at different points in the calendar. If you have not heard anything from a school (no rejection, waiting list, or acceptance) by about March 1st, a call to the school or the director of the admission process would be recommended. Popular schools receive a large number of applications and do not always notify the rejected applications. In fact, they may not even contact you if a part of your application is missing, so do not be afraid to call and inquire as to whether anything is missing or whether there is additional information that the admissions committee might need to make their decision. Over the years, we have seen many qualified students fail to be considered because their admissions package was missing a single piece of data, such as one letter of recommendation.

Even if your dream school gives you a great offer early in the process, we would advise against accepting it right away. A rational approach to decision making is scientifically sound, so take some time to think through your options and talk about the offers with your family and friends. Many I-O programs have subscribed to the April 15th resolution (see Textbox 6.1 below), which gives programs a common deadline for prospective students' acceptances. Those institutions that are not part of the resolution may have slightly earlier deadlines.

TEXTBOX 6.1 APRIL 15TH RESOLUTION

Many I-O graduate programs have signed on to the Resolution of Graduate Scholars, Fellows, Trainees, and Assistants created by the Council of Graduate Schools. This specifies that students offered graduate scholarships or assistantships are not required to respond to offers prior to *April 15th*. Having a common deadline can help navigate the process of weighing your offers more easily. You can find the full resolution and institutions that have expressed support online.

When you receive an offer, you should clarify when official responses are needed from each program and take the time you need, within those time frames, to consider your choices or wait for other responses. Honesty and transparency are highly valued among admissions committees; you need to look out for your best interest first, but you can also be considerate by declining offers you know are not viable options and checking in with programs to let them know where you are with your personal decision-making process.

While you are evaluating your options, you should be gathering as much information as possible about each of your offers to help you make the right choice. Try to fill in any gaps so that you can make a fair and fully informed comparison among your offers; if you were invited to an interview day where you visited with one program but not another, you should see if a program visit is an option or whether you might be able to have a video conference with program faculty.

FOLLOWING THE MONEY

Although some schools offer scholarships or fellowships, for most traditional Ph.D. programs, your acceptance will come along with a graduate assistantship package. Master's programs are less likely to provide assistantships but may offer some types of tuition remission or wavier. Some applicants will choose to follow the money and accept the offer with the best-paying assistantship; we would caution students against this simple choice, as with most matters in life you should always read the contract and the fine print carefully.

Truly comparing the financial implications of different programs involves so much more than one number. Offers with the same quoted dollar amount are not always equal. An assistantship that also comes with a tuition waiver, often called tuition remission, has to be weighted quite differently than one where you have to pay tuition and fees out of your own pocket. Table 6.2 illustrates how even offers that appear to be the same in terms of dollars, can result in very different amounts of value to the graduate student.

In addition, you could be comparing assistantship packages from all over the country, or even in different countries, in locations with vastly different costs of living, and more appealing offers may come along with much higher rent payments. Do your own research as to cost of living for different geographic areas and talk with current students about how they make their finances work and whether it is common to supplement assistantships with extra work or student loans.

Additional considerations are the type of work expected of you in your assistantship: *will you be grading exams in a completely different department, or working on research in your advisor's lab?* Taking an assistantship with work that is related to your future goals might be worth having slightly less income. Graduate assistantships tend to follow the nine-month academic calendar, so you should also look into whether summer funding is offered and what type of work is entailed. Finally, things like the cost of student fees certainly should not be a main concern but will help you get a full picture of the academic expenses you will take on.

Also, be wary of offers that do not provide you with an assistantship but that tell you that if you perform well in the first year, you might be awarded an assistantship in your second year; such offers may never materialize. Similarly, inquire as to whether the assistantship is guaranteed

Table 6.2 Value of Different Assistantship Offers

Quoted Offer Per Year	Stipend – Paid as Salary	Yearly Tuition Cost	Tuition Remission Offered with Assistantship	Tuition Paid Out-of-Pocket Yearly
$40,000	$20,000	$20,000	Yes	0
$20,000	$20,000	$20,000	Yes	0
$20,000	$20,000	$20,000	No	$20,000
$20,000	$20,000	$40,000	No	$40,000
$30,000	$20,000	$20,000	Half	$10,000

for all the years that will be required to complete the program. Otherwise, you may be looking for funding on your own in your second year. Although more common with law schools than psychology programs, exercise caution if your assistantship is dependent upon maintaining a certain level of successful performance, in terms of GPA or relative ranking in the program. In Table 6.3, we review some of the other factors you should be cognizant of in comparing offers from programs.

When it comes down to it, life and graduate school are both expensive. Finances will be an issue in pursuing an advanced degree. Completing a graduate program is stressful and becomes all the more difficult if you are

---

Table 6.3 Comparing Different Assistantship Offers – Questions to Ask

Regarding the assistantship in general:

- Is this an assistantship, scholarship, or fellowship?
- Is it guaranteed for the first year?
- Is it guaranteed for all the years I am in the program?
- What will I have to do to retain the assistantship? Can I lose it depending upon my GPA or class ranking?

Regarding the monetary stipend:

- What is the dollar amount of stipend being offered?
- Is the stipend for nine months or for 12 months?
- If it is a nine-month stipend, are there opportunities for additional funding in the summer?
- Do I have to do work for the stipend?
- Will I be doing teaching, research, or something else? Will I be working in the psychology department or elsewhere on campus?
- How many hours per week do I have to work?
- Who will my supervisor be?
- Can I do other paid work?

Regarding the tuition waiver or remission:

- Is there a tuition remission? What does it cover?
- Does it cover fees? What should I still expect to pay?

Other benefits:

- Do I get medical insurance?
- Do I have to pay taxes and social security?

struggling to pay your rent and to eat. You could take on an extra job, but that would cut into study time. Or you could take out loans, but those need to be repaid eventually. It is up to you to carefully consider how you will balance your budget including your income and expenses.

LOCATION

If circumstances allow, it is best to be flexible and open to different geographical regions and cities. Sure, a school in the mountains would allow the option of close to year-round skiing, and who among us has not dreamed of studying on a beach listening to the ocean waves. However, historically many of the earliest and best I-O programs have been in the so-called "Big Ten" area, which encompasses much of the Midwest and in part explains the origin of the phrase "dust-bowl" empiricism. At The University of Akron, many of our graduate students originate from California and Florida. Adapting when attending school in Ohio, Michigan, or Minnesota for someone from the South may lead to some humorous adventures, like your first time driving in snow. But the advantage is you will not mind being in your office collecting research data and studying for 12 hours a day as you're not missing much outdoors.

You might not be thrilled at the thought of relocating, or at the possibility of living in a college town or a new city far from home, but remember that you are investing in an education that will afford you greater opportunities in the future. So, while it is certainly something to consider, we would put location at the very bottom of the list below other potential factors. And you never know, you may end up liking a place you never thought you would.

In considering locations with an open mind, you should think of a few things that are "deal breakers" for you. If possible, take a visit to the cities or towns you are considering and consider whether you can see yourself living there. If you have a well-developed support system in your hometown that you need for your psychological health and well-being, then moving across the country might not be the right choice. Just remember that graduate school is only temporary; well, at least for most it is, unless you end up on the 15-year plan.

FIT WITH FACULTY AND STUDENTS

Program culture is an important part of the graduate school experience and it could be a deciding factor between two similar offers. Introduce yourself to a prospective faculty mentor, talk a bit about your ideas and goals, and ask about their mentoring style. As we will discuss further in Chapter 7, your relationship with your advisor is probably the most important one in graduate school. If one of your target schools has a faculty member who is working on projects that really interest you, and you find it easy to exchange ideas with this scholar, this is a good indicator of what can turn into a positive, productive working relationship.

You will want to get a good sense of the overall climate or culture of the program, to do this, you should speak with current students and ask questions about their day-to-day schedule, how they approach course-work, deal with advisors, and work with one another. Determine what it would be like to be a student in that program and whether the program culture seems appealing to you. Getting several different perspectives can start to put the complete picture together for you.

Some schools are hyper-competitive, with students competing for the top grades and the best assistantships and internships. Other schools offer a more laid back, less intensive experience. *Is a highly competitive environment one that will motivate you?* Some people prefer working alone and might excel in a more competitive program, others may rely on social support and teamwork to get through challenging semesters and would be a better fit in more collaborative programs. Some programs are highly structured, with all students taking all the same courses in the same temporal order. Other programs offer almost complete freedom of choice, while in others your program of study will be determined by your advisor or a faculty committee of your choosing. *Do you prefer more structure or more choice?*

Consideration should be given to the diversity of the faculty, graduate students, the school, and the geographical area associated with each pro-gram. We believe issues of diversity are relevant to everyone, but especially those who identify with any underrepresented group. *Is there a faculty member who would understand your experience as a person and a graduate student? Are there other graduate students who share your views or interests? If you are a religious person, is there a church or synagogue that reflects your faith in the area?*

Well-meaning faculty will try to be supportive to the unique needs of different students, but representation is something that cannot be forced and I-O still has a long way to go to show that it fully embraces the value of diversity. Although I-O programs are fairly gender-balanced in terms of both graduate students and faculty, there may be gender differences in faculty rank and promotion status. The representation of racial and ethnic minorities in I-O is still much lower than desirable. The adjustment to graduate school is tough, so whether a program offers sources of community and support, especially within the faculty, should be a question of high priority.

RANKINGS

Program quality and reputation are definitely important, but not are not easily quantified. Doing a Google search for I-O graduate program rankings might lead you down a never-ending rabbit hole. For program rankings that are done systematically based on different criteria, we would look to SIOP, which does graduate program rankings every few years. We recommend browsing the SIOP rankings to see which programs are consistently highly ranked across the board, or stand out in a certain area. If you have academic aspirations, rankings based on research productivity would be especially informative. For others, applied developmental opportunities or program resources might be more salient criteria.

TEXTBOX 6.2 SIOP RANKINGS

One source of I-O Psychology graduate program rankings can be found in *The Industrial-Organizational Psychologist* (*TIP*). *TIP* is a publication put out by SIOP which has taken on the initiative of generating rankings based on thorough and transparent processes. At this time, Volume 55(4) contains the most recent rankings, which you will see vary based upon the indicators used.

With that said, do not put too much faith in a specific number or ranking. You should be able to talk to people who can elaborate on the overall reputation of a certain program in the field, teaching and research opportunities, and the productivity of certain labs. We find these conversations to add important context to the numbers.

Hopefully, you have already checked out the backgrounds and interests of the departmental and area faculty. In addition to any information on the university website, a Google Scholar search can be performed on the individual faculty to gather information on their latest and most important publications. If the faculty member has activated their account in Google Scholar, the search will also provide you with an h-index, which is an indicator of the impact of the professor on the field.

TEXTBOX 6.3 GOOGLE SCHOLAR SEARCH

Get familiar with doing research on faculty using Google Scholar searches. Go to https://scholar.google.com/. Type Dennis Doverspike and hit return. You should find a profile and a list of publications for Dennis Doverspike. On the right side of the page, you will find various indicators of citation frequency, including the h-index, which is based on the number of publications and the number of citations per publication. Now try entering a few other names, perhaps the names of faculty at a school you are interested in attending.

We would also caution that by their very nature, rankings are often dated. A highly ranked Ph.D. program may not be admitting any students this year because the university has cut graduate funding. Rankings for master's program tend to vary more across time than do Ph.D. reputations. In part, this is because Ph.D. programs usually have larger faculties. A master's program may only have two core faculty, one with an industrial concentration and one in the organizational area. If one or both of those faculty leave, it will have a significant impact on the master's program ability to admit students and offer courses.

MASTER'S OR PH.D.?

Hopefully, by this point you have already made this decision. However, it is still one of the most common questions we hear. You should go back to those critical questions such as whether you want an applied career or one in academia. If you are leaning toward working in an applied setting, but still want to keep your options open, then a Ph.D. program might be a better fit. Think about whether you are eager to get into the workforce quickly, or are willing to invest in a longer degree path. If four to six years of more schooling does not appeal to you, then a master's might be the better choice.

This does bring up an additional point worth considering: *If you are admitted into a terminal master's program at a university with a Ph.D. program, is there any possibility of switching into the Ph.D. sequence? On the other hand, if you are admitted into a Ph.D. program, and find it is not what you wanted, can you leave with a master's degree?* These are important questions you will want to address with the program faculty.

WHAT TO DO IF YOU ARE PLACED ON A WAITING LIST?

What should you do if you are put on a waiting list? Wait!

Seriously, the answer depends on your other offers. Schools often receive rejections from the first set of offers they give, and then turn to the waiting list. However, those rejections may not be received until April 15th. This can put you in the uncomfortable position of having an offer in hand from a school that might be a second-choice, while sitting on the waiting list of a first-choice school. Of course, there is the old adage "a bird in the hand is worth two in the bush."

In reality, this is one of the more difficult and challenging dilemmas an applicant may face. However you choose to deal with this situation, it should be handled in an ethical, responsible, transparent, and professional manner. Any contractual issues aside, no one wants someone to enter their program unhappy because the student could have gone somewhere else. You want to be fair to yourself as well as the other parties involved by making sure you select the right program.

WHAT TO DO IF YOU DO NOT GET AN OFFER?

You may not get any offers in your first application cycle. We can understand being upset and disappointed if all you receive is rejection letters; it is a setback. If this happens, take some time to consider what the weak areas in your application were and what you can do to address them in the future, either by improving in a certain area or applying to different programs that are a better match.

Your weakness could be something obvious to you, such as a poor GRE score or very little research experience, but, if not, you can reach out to admissions committees and ask what would make for a stronger application. Once you have identified the weak points in your application, you can start creating an action plan for remedying those areas. Or, maybe you applied to the wrong programs and need to reconsider your choice of potential schools or degree options. If you have a trusted faculty member mentor, this would be a great time to sit down with your undergraduate advisor and consider possible alternatives.

A lot of people in this situation will take a year or two to work in HR before reapplying to graduate programs. If you can find a job that supports your life goals, you might be better equipped to handle graduate school when you do get that offer because of your previous work experience. Another possibility would be to dedicate your time to pursuing research or even to assisting a faculty member with a research study that could lead to a publication. If you only applied to schools offering a Ph.D., you may still have time to apply for and be admitted to a terminal master's or MBA program.

*****

We hope that this discussion of decisions has been helpful rather than overwhelming. There are many factors to consider because finding the right fit in a graduate program is a decision that should not be taken lightly. Think about what matters most to you and how that aligns with the values and culture presented in the different programs you are considering, but also keep logistics such as finances, location, and school-life balance in mind. If you fail to receive an offer the first time around, you can seek some constructive feedback on what you can do to strengthen applications the next time around, or realign your expectations so that you have a higher probability of acceptance during your next round of applications.

THE GRADUATE STUDENT YEARS

CHAPTER 7

The Graduate School Years

This chapter is meant to be a high-level overview of the ins and outs of graduate school in I-O Psychology. Graduate school is most certainly a busy and stressful phase in one's career, but you will find a lot of I-O professionals look back fondly on their graduate school days and stay connected with the people they met in their program for many years. We hope to provide some insight into what graduate school is like, how to be successful in graduate school, and how to deal with important choices. We do this by tackling common questions like:

- What courses should I take?
- How do I choose and deal with an advisor?
- What is a master's thesis?
- What is a doctoral dissertation?
- When should I start networking and attending conferences?
- How do I find balance with school and my personal life?

As discussed in Chapter 5, there are a variety of degree and program types, but we focus on traditional M.A. or M.A./Ph.D. programs, which are the typical experience for most I-O practitioners. A unique perspective on life and happiness in graduate school is offered in our donated story by Katya Caravella, which appears in Table 7.1.

COURSES

As a graduate student, you may not have much of a choice in what courses you take, since requirements and course offerings are often planned by the faculty or dictated by program requirements. If you do have discretion as

Table 7.1 Katya Caravella, M.A., Learning to Survive and Thrive in Graduate School

I first learned about I-O Psychology in college, during a brief module about the subject in an introductory Psychology class. It fascinated me because it brought to light so many opportunities for change in the world of work, a world in which we spend the majority of our lives. Having people close to me begrudgingly talk about various aspects of their work experiences made me believe that there must be an alternative to feeling dissatisfied for 40+ hours a week. I felt drawn to the field as a result, because it showed promise for empowering employees to take ownership of their situations and move toward positive change. And I really wanted to be part of that possibility.

Upon graduating college, I pursued a master's degree in I-O. I was set on a master's program versus a Ph.D. program for a few reasons. The first being, very honestly, my impatience. Being so fascinated by what I was learning, I wanted to soak up all the relevant information I could and use it in the "real world" as soon as I learned it. And at the time, the master's program seemed to fulfill the applied nature of this science more so than the Ph.D. track. I was eager to step into the role of an I-O practitioner and was far more interested in the creative problem-solving process utilizing I-O research, rather than being involved in the research itself.

I completed my master's at the beginning of Summer in 2017 and embarked on a life adventure within the same month when I moved to Colorado. I did some instructional design and SJT item-writing contract work while job-searching. I was fortunate to quickly land a job as a contract HR Generalist with Northwood Investors, which turned into a permanent position within a couple of months. I now work as an HR Project Specialist for this rapidly growing real estate investment firm, where I get to apply my I-O knowledge and skills while managing the payroll and benefit administration, performance review redesign, compensation system design, HR data management, and organizational policy revision efforts.

Thinking back to how graduate school prepared me for my current role, one of the most valuable parts of my experience happened at the tail-end of the program, as I was studying for the specialty exam. This process forced me to integrate materials from all my classes and mentally organize themes and research findings in a way that made the concepts more tangible. We spend so much time diving into the details of the research, that taking a "bird's eye view" and figuring out the many ways the cross-topic research could apply in a real-world context cannot be understated. As a result, this integration of different I-O topics prepared me to think about workforce challenges in a broader perspective. It emphasized the crucial part that context plays in such situations. Rarely does factor A clearly have an effect on factor B without something else influencing the relationship.

In industry, you are challenged to figure out which findings and methods are likely to be the most useful based on the context of the issue you are trying to resolve. I am learning in my current role that there is no "cookie cutter" approach that fits all situations. And although this kind of uncertainty can bring about discomfort, this is exactly the right opportunity to exercise the solid critical thinking skills we tend to develop during our graduate school years. I am also learning that a single business decision doesn't exist in a vacuum. Whether it is a policy change, a new on-boarding program design, or a compensation structure redesign, these decisions tend to have ripple effects on other aspects of the organization. I've found this to be a valuable insight that keeps my work exciting and meaningful.

The best advice I can give to others in pursuit of success in graduate school is to seek experiences that force you to bring I-O concepts to life in a material way. In other words, I cannot emphasize the value of internships, consulting work, and opportunities that allow you to lead group projects enough. I personally found projects such as validity assessment, training program design, creation of competency-based interview questions, adverse impact analysis, and survey design to be incredibly effective tools to integrate I-O research and create work projects I can reference down the road. Having resources at hand with which you are familiar can save a lot of time and frustration when working on I-O or HR-related projects. Keeping my graduate school materials and project deliverables organized has already served me very well in my current job. I could not be more grateful for the challenges and growth opportunities that my role affords me on a daily basis, and the experiences that prepared me to get here.

to when you can take certain courses, we recommend taking courses as early as possible, as it will be much easier to deal with a larger course load early on, than to try to make classes work around internships and other obligations that arise for advanced graduate students. Our general advice would be not to feel limited by the courses offered in your graduate program. If you are interested in a topic that your program does not offer a course in, find a free online course and get a group of graduate students to work on it together and talk through problems as a team.

Graduate level courses are likely very different from the lecture-based courses that are more typical at the undergraduate level. There is usually a large amount of reading material, and we do mean large as in sometimes hundreds of pages for each class meeting, and class sessions are primarily based on discussions about the readings. This requires organization so that you can distribute your reading throughout a longer time span, rather than rushing through articles the night before a class meeting. Within your courses, take advantage of the resources you have in your fellow graduate students, although you may also find you get more out of working independently. Students might find courses more manageable when they work together to create study guides or outlines, study for exams as a group, and talk through everyone's understanding of certain problems or theories.

Grades in graduate school are important. Many programs consider any grade below a B to be evidence of a failure to master the work. However, receiving top grades in graduate school is expected and you should be wary of devoting too many of your resources to obtaining the highest grade in the class, as in many programs a greater emphasis is placed on research productivity than on grades.

TEXTBOX 7.1 PH.D. COMICS

Graduate school is more bearable when you do not take yourself too seriously. *Piled Higher and Deeper* is a great comic that pokes fun at the idiosyncrasies of the academic life. Check it out at: www.phdcomics.com/.

GRADUATE ASSISTANTSHIPS

Hopefully, you will receive some type of graduate assistantship or financial assistantship. If you have a research assistantship, you should be very happy, as your life has become easier. You will be paid to be involved in research that will further your career.

If you received a teaching assistantship, it may be a very new experience for you. In some cases, you may be younger than the under-graduate students you are teaching. This could turn out to be an advantage as students may give you high ratings because they identify with you, or you may struggle with asserting yourself as an expert in the course material. Luckily, there are many faculty and other graduate students who can help you with your teaching. Most likely, you will have some materials to draw from that have been handed down by other graduate students, which will make your preparation easier. If the thought of teaching college courses intimidates you, know that comfort and composure with teaching really does come easily with experience, and we have seen so many graduate students transform from nervous wrecks on their first day in front of a classroom to cool, calm, and collected effective instructors.

Although teaching is not your main focus in graduate school, you should do a good and competent job. It is important to come to class prepared. Maintaining an energetic and confident attitude with your students will go a long way. However, we would again encourage balance and remind you that the emphasis of many programs is on research. The main goal is to find your ideal distribution of time spent on classes, teaching, and conducting and publishing high-quality research.

ADVISORS AND RESEARCH

Pairing graduate students with advisors is often the first thing that admissions committees work on, and as an incoming graduate student, the advisor you would be working with is one of the most important aspects of your decision. Your primary concern should be whether there is a match as far as your research interests.

Regardless of whether you want a career in academia or in industry, doctoral programs and certain master's programs have a heavy emphasis on research, and your advisor is usually expected to include you in their research efforts or research lab. You should be clear as to what you are interested in and able to work on, and always make sure your primary focus is on your thesis or dissertation. At the same time, if you want to obtain one of the top jobs after graduation, it is important to try to present research at conferences and submit articles to high-quality journal outlets. Make your goals clear and your advisor should be willing to work with you to achieve your research goals.

Every advisor is different, and it would be a good idea to have an early conversation about working styles and expectations, so you are not caught off guard. If any conflict arises, do your best to manage it in a mature and proactive way, as this is one of the most important relationships in graduate school and your future career. Your advisor might help you find your first job, and many students continue publishing with their advisor for many years after graduate school.

Students' research interests often develop and change throughout graduate school; you should feel free to explore other areas and collaborate on projects with other faculty and graduate students. If you want to completely change your primary research focus, many graduate students switch advisors if there is another faculty member in the department that would be a better match. However, this can be dependent on the philosophy of the program, as some are very advisor-centric and discourage changing advisors. In some cases, graduate students end up changing universities completely to find an advisor that they can work with in a professional and productive fashion. Ultimately, you need to figure out your needs and work to have a mutually beneficial relationship with an advisor that will help you attain your goals.

CAPSTONE EXAMS

Most I-O professionals would agree that the process of studying for and taking some capstone exam, which may be called a qualifying exam or comprehensive exam, was a huge part of their graduate school experience. This is an exam that is typically structured either as a final requirement for graduation at the end of a master's program, or a milestone between the thesis and dissertation in doctoral programs. We find that different programs design this exam in so many different ways that it would be impossible for us to provide a realistic preview of what or how to study here. What we can say is that in general, students should spend about six months preparing by studying research in all major content areas of I-O Psychology, and then sit for the exam using the knowledge base of an I-O generalist to answer questions and solve problems.

We encourage students to collect information on the requirements for capstone exams so that they have a realistic idea of what their graduate school experience will look like. However, we caution against lending a lot of weight to this factor or worrying about the exam at such an early stage. When the time comes to prepare for the exam, you will already have accumulated a great deal of I-O knowledge, effective study and organization strategies, and tips and tricks from older graduate students.

THESIS

All Ph.D. students and some master's students will need to complete a thesis, which is an original research project that contributes to the I-O literature. We recommend you get started on this as early as possible, as procrastinating on this can easily lead to problems down the road, and can even delay your graduation. Completing your thesis will be a collaborative project with your advisor, and advisors will differ to the extent that they will guide your topic area or encourage you to use a certain method that fits in with their ongoing work.

Either way, once you identify a topic you are interested in, dedicate yourself to reading as many academic articles as you can about the area, including review pieces, theoretical papers, and empirical studies. Focus on the conclusions, limitations, and future research questions, which will help stimulate ideas for what the unanswered questions are and how you might fill in those knowledge gaps. Typically, the goal is to design a study, which could be survey-based or experimental, that will expand upon or clarify an existing issue in the literature. You might be working on this before you have taken a course in research methods, in which case you will have to rely on your advisor to ensure your study design is sound. Make sure you are clear on an analytic strategy ahead of time so that you can have an idea of whether you will need to familiarize yourself with a new technique or software program.

TEXTBOX 7.2 THESIS IDEAS

Some of our best ideas come to us at unexpected times. You might figure out a great way to restructure your thesis in the middle of the night, and then fall asleep and forget it. We recommend graduate students make a habit of always keeping a notebook close, paper and pencil or electronic, to jot down those ideas whenever they come to you.

For many graduate students, the thesis is the first time that they are working on a project that is this large in scope and with this level of independence. Most individuals make their way to graduate school because they know how to do well in structured classes. When confronted with the lack of clarity and deadlines inherent in a thesis or dissertation, the normally competent student becomes flummoxed. There is a reason some professors will tell you the most important skill in graduate school is "tolerance for ambiguity."

The whole process of an independent research project like the thesis can be overwhelming for some, and we recommend self-imposing a structure to break this down into smaller pieces. Schedule regular meetings with your advisor and establish internal deadlines for when you want to have certain papers read and sections written. Certain parts of this process will be out of your hands, such as how long it takes for committees to read your drafts, but for the most part you are in control of how the project moves along if you are willing to put in the work.

DISSERTATION

Successfully completing a doctoral dissertation is typically the final step in attaining your Ph.D. The terms "thesis" and "dissertation" are used interchangeably in some fields, but the main difference is that you are expected to work on the dissertation as a more advanced graduate student. As such, there are higher standards for the caliber of the research you propose and the potential contribution to the field. This involves a more comprehensive literature review, with firm grounding in an area of research, and may involve conceptualizing a new construct or integrating theoretical perspectives in a model. You will need to form a committee of faculty members who are familiar with your research project and can evaluate your work and offer feedback in a proposal and defense.

For most graduate students, the dissertation is the most extensive project they have taken on, and the work is highly independent and self-driven from the beginning of your research question until the defense. This can seem daunting, but you will have several years of experience under your belt that have prepared you for this work. Plus, in whatever topic you undertake, almost no one in the world will have more expertise than you will when you finish.

At the same time, your place as an advanced graduate student can work as a double-edged sword in the dissertation process. Although you have more content knowledge and project management experience than your earlier years in your graduate program, you are also more focused on your next steps after graduate school. You may be pursuing an internship or even a full-time job while working on your dissertation, which is a challenge for even those with the best time-management skills. It will take a great deal of commitment and planning to complete a dissertation project.

TEXTBOX 7.3 THE DISSERTATION

Completing a dissertation is a challenging task, but the use of effective tools and strategies will make it more manageable. Many of our colleagues have found this book to be helpful in identifying some of those strategies: *Demystifying Dissertation Writing: A Streamlined Process from Choice of Topic to Final Text* by Peg Boyle Single, Ph.D.

It may help to break down the project into smaller milestones and set goals for each of those achievements. We see the main milestones as: writing the first draft of your dissertation proposal, successfully proposing your dissertation to a committee of faculty members, collecting data, analyzing data, and successfully defending the dissertation to your committee.

You will probably learn and abhor the abbreviation *ABD*, which stands for *All But Dissertation*. The unfortunate reality is that too many Ph.D. students never finish their dissertation and do not obtain their degree, taking on a permanent *ABD* status (See Chapter 8 on internships and ABD status). Often this is because they are already working and simply cannot find the time to complete such a demanding task. However, this does not have to be the case for those that want or need to pursue a job, and we have seen some creative ways to get it done, like "weekend sprints" (i.e., isolating yourself in a workspace from Saturday morning to Sunday night with snacks and a clear writing goal) and "dissercations" (i.e., taking a trip to a tropical island to work on your next draft on the beach).

NETWORKING

The relationships you form with fellow graduate students and faculty in your graduate program will be incredibly valuable for your career. Throughout your time as a graduate student, faculty in your program will see your growth and development, you will have plenty of opportunities to make a good impression through things like contributing to class discussion, giving presentations, and collaborating on projects. Do not be afraid to use these connections when the time comes to get on the job market.

Networking outside of your department may be even more important to your career goals, and we believe attending conferences is the best way to organically meet professionals in the field. We often hear stories about people landing their first job or gaining access to a great data collection opportunity because of someone they met at a SIOP happy hour. Try to attend conferences as early on as possible to get an idea of what they are like and how to navigate the environment. The largest gatherings in I-O are the annual SIOP conference and the annual Academy of Management conference, although there are smaller gatherings as well based on region or research focus, plus specialty conferences for graduate students.

There are several approaches you can take to networking, from informally approaching a more established person after a talk they give or at a social gathering, to making a connection in more structured environments like speed mentoring sessions or committee meetings. You should try to meet somebody that you could potentially have a mutually beneficial relationship with, so spend some time thinking about what you might have to offer or share with someone in a more successful position than you are currently. You may have an idea about some future research, access to a certain sample, or a special skill. We think that the most successful networking comes from going into it with an open mind and engaging in conversations with the goal to learn about different people's experiences and careers. At the same time, you should put your best foot forward and carry yourself in a professional manner.

LIFE BALANCE

Ironically, I-O graduate students are not always the best at practicing what we learn about stress and well-being at work. Taking a proactive approach to balancing your responsibilities will help you be as productive and happy as possible. Many graduate students will take on part-time jobs for financial reasons. Our experience is if you take a job not related to the field, work can easily start to interfere with how much time you can dedicate to your studies. Especially for doctoral students, we would advise against working outside of your department assignments or suggest limiting work to no more than ten hours a week. You want to fully dedicate yourself to graduate school as it is an investment in your future career.

Between coursework, teaching, research, and internships, life gets busy in graduate school. Many of us have struggled in the transition to graduate level work because the nature of it is much more ambiguous and fluid; we remind you that the most important skill to develop in graduate school is "tolerance for ambiguity." In your undergraduate years, you mainly focus on securing an "A" in your courses. In graduate school, you work on projects like a master's thesis without a clear rubric. You may enjoy being able to make your own schedule, or feel you are always falling behind without those strict deadlines. Once you find a routine that works for you it will get easier, whether it is working from home on days you do not have class or creating meeting times with your cohort to hold each other accountable for studying at certain times.

If you are just starting graduate school, one helpful suggestion is to scaffold your responsibilities, meaning progressively adding to your workload. To do this, we would suggest when you first get to graduate school, determine how much time you need for your classes and studies, as well as any assistantship duties. Once you find out how well you can handle classes and your department responsibilities, then start to think about approaching professors regarding greater involvement in research. Or, consider becoming involved in practical experience, internships, or consulting. Find out what you can handle and then gradually add additional tasks.

TEXTBOX 7.4 GOALS

Keep it simple! When in graduate school, it might seem that your to-do list is never-ending. Break up your list into more manageable pieces. Committing to just two or three main goals each day will help you work toward your long term goals in a more efficient, productive fashion.

Self-care is an important part of success in graduate school. You may find yourself busier than ever before, but you should make a point to plan breaks and celebrate even small milestones. Make time for activities and hobbies outside of graduate school as well. If you relocate for a graduate program, being in a new city may bring about feelings of isolation. Joining a group with a common interest can be a great way to socialize and meet new people.

*****

Graduate school can be the best years of your life; you will make lifelong friends, you will become an expert in a specialized area of study, and you will accomplish things you did not think were possible. Of course, from day one, you should also be planning to make yourself competitive for your future job opportunities. The best ways to do this are to impress your faculty in your courses, to actively engage in research, and to present your findings at conferences and in journal publications. Make the most of it because before you know it, graduate school will be over and you will be applying for jobs.

CHAPTER 8

Applied Experience and Internships

If your goal is to land an applied job after graduate school, whether you want to work in industry, consulting, or have no idea what type of work you enjoy, doing an applied internship is a great way to gain work experience and refine future goals. Even if your plan is to obtain a top academic job at a Ph.D. granting institution, we would advise obtaining practical experience. This chapter deals with internships, giving our perspective on common issues like:

* Do I need to do an internship?
* How do I get an internship?
* How should I prepare for interviews?
* How can I find success in my internship?
* Can I be too successful in an internship?

Throughout this book, many of our contributors describe how their internship experience was critical in obtaining their first job. In Table 8.1, Tyler Slezak describes his recent search for a position, the onboarding experience, and experience as an intern in an external consulting firm.

INTERNSHIPS

We would argue that if you are offered an I-O internship while in graduate school, you should absolutely take it. If you are unsure as to whether you want to go academic or applied, getting this experience can help you make that decision. We have also seen students say they want to work at a big company in an internal role from day one, then switch to

Table 8.1 Tyler Slezak, M.A., Searching for and Obtaining an Internship

In my third year of my Ph.D. in I-O Psychology at The University of Akron, I knew I wanted to pursue an applied career. To hone my skillset in an applied context, I decided it was important to find an internship. Fortunately, a company specializing in developing selection assessments, Shaker International, Inc., is local to Northeast Ohio. Akron's I-O program has a strong relationship with Shaker, with many Akron alumni working as full-time consultants and a few current students working as interns. I researched Shaker and talked to a few of their interns to gain a better understanding of the work they do. The work seemed innovative and intriguing, and I was particularly impressed by the type of clients Shaker was working with. I discussed my interest in Shaker with my department chair, Dr. Paul Levy, and he was able to arrange an interview at Shaker for me. A week after my interview, I was offered a position as a member of the Innovation team. I accepted the offer and began my internship while entering the fourth year of my Ph.D.

Shaker specializes in developing pre-employment selection assessments, known as Virtual Job Tryouts ® (VJTs). VJTs are multi-method assessments that use a combination of personality, work history, situational judgment, and work sample simulations to predict a candidate's job fit. VJTs also provide candidates with information about job demands and company culture. This facilitates a two-way information exchange, so both the candidate and the organization can evaluate fit and compatibility. Shaker has developed VJTs in a variety of industries, including call centers, retail, banking, and health care.

I joined Shaker at a time when a key initiative was to expand the off-the-shelf or Standard VJT catalog. Historically, Shaker has partnered with clients to make Custom VJTs, which are customized to the client's brand and role they are hiring for. The tailoring and specifications required for a Custom VJT means the development process is time-intensive. Some clients are not looking for this level of specification and prefer a more ready-to-use hiring solution. For these clients, an off-the-shelf Standard VJT is a more desirable product. My primary role when I started as an R&D intern was assisting in the development of Standard VJTs.

To develop Standard VJTs, I reviewed job analyses and validation studies from previously developed Custom VJTs. After reviewing these studies, I consolidated data on content and predictive validity. This data helped determine the measurement exercises used in Standard VJTs. Along with other members of the R&D team, I considered predictive validity, job relevance, and adverse impact of each exercise when deciding if it should be included in a Standard VJT. Each Standard VJT is paired with a Test Manual, and I created many of these by compiling evidence from previous predictive validity studies, relevant findings from selection research, job relevance of VJT exercises, and best practices for using the VJT based on recommendations from SIOP, *The Uniform Guidelines*, and the

EEOC. It was my job to present this information in a way that clients understood exactly what they were getting in a Standard VJT and how to best implement the VJT in their organization.

In addition to assisting in the development of Standard VJTs, I have worked as part of a team creating Custom VJTs. One of the first steps is this is a comprehensive job analysis of the position. A large part of my role on Custom VJT projects was assisting with job analysis activities. Shaker takes a multi-method approach to job analysis, including a Job Analysis Questionnaire (JAQ) completed by incumbents, focus groups with incumbents, job observations, and interviews with managers and HR professionals who have line of site to the position's future state. I managed JAQ data and presented the results in technical reports, led focus groups, and observed incumbents performing the job we were developing a VJT for. Additionally, I assisted in summarizing the data from all job analysis efforts. This data is used as the foundation for creating the exercise content of a Custom VJT.

I believe this internship will benefit my future career in several ways. First, this internship has given me the opportunity to directly apply the knowledge and skills I developed in graduate school. Many of the steps and processes for developing a VJT align with what I learned in my Selection, Test and Measurement, and Individual Assessment courses. At the same time, I have gained a more comprehensive understanding of how selection assessments are built and implemented. Second, while interning at Shaker I learned the importance of customer service in consulting work. Shaker provides their clients much more than a product, they provide a client-oriented experience and serve as a trusted advisor to all their clients. Prior to my internship, I had not considered this aspect of consulting work. Being a trusted advisor, stronger client relationships are formed, which can lead to continued and future partnerships. Finally, I have a better understanding of how to articulate the value of I-O Psychology. Through sitting in on client calls and playing a part in producing technical reports and manuals, I have gained invaluable insight to what clients care about when it comes to the services we provide them.

consulting after doing an internal internship. Even if you are committed to a career in academia, we would argue that an internship experience can help in your teaching endeavors by giving you familiarity with the practice side of I-O.

Why? Well, it is human nature to change our minds; students who enter graduate school pledging to enter the professorate, may find in their last year in school, or maybe even a few years into the first academic job that they would enjoy an applied job more than the ivory tower. More critically, we believe all academics should have some practical experience. Engaging in an internship can provide "war stories" with which to pepper one's lectures, which is especially important if you end up as a professor in a business school. Most programs at the Ph.D. level require that students complete some type of internship; thus, those institutions look for faculty who can supervise students in internships. At the master's level, the ability of faculty to supervise practical work by students is even more critical.

If seeking a non-academic position, your future employers want to hire motivated candidates who have demonstrated the ability to do the type of work they are applying for, even if their experience is on a smaller scale. Internships will help you develop the competencies needed for your future job; as we all know, it is one thing to read about and study a topic, but a very different experience to apply your knowledge out in the real world.

It will prove challenging to land a first job if you lack any internship experience, so gaining applied skill is something you should prioritize. As a general rule, yes, you should take an internship if you have the opportunity to do so. But there are exceptions to every rule, as not all intern experiences are the same, and it is important to find a good fit in an internship that is both developmental and allows you to maintain balance with your other roles and responsibilities.

There are also different types of internships and similar types may have different names or titles (See Table 8.2). Regardless of the exact type, it is important that you find a way to document having experience in organizational settings and that you can demonstrate competence in applying the skills associated with your I-O knowledge base.

FINDING AN INTERNSHIP

Internship applications can be competitive, and this is one area in which programs vary widely in the available opportunities. Some I-O programs, especially master's programs, have internship requirements; those programs have most likely established connections with local organizations that tend to consider their students for positions. On the other hand, you could find yourself in a doctoral program in which faculty are not as well-connected in the business world, and may not be able to help as much in your search. So, depending on the program, you might have your top choice of an internship pretty much lined up for you, you could be on your own browsing online postings and job fairs for openings, or land somewhere in between. This is certainly something you can consider when applying for graduate programs, but either way, finding an internship should be attainable if you go about it thoughtfully.

Table 8.2 Types of Practical Experience[a]

Label	Paid or Unpaid	Duration	Level	Description
Post-Doctoral Internship	Paid	1 year, 40 hours per week	Post-Ph.D.	A formal work agreement with an external organization. Usually paid directly to the individual. Completed after completing the Ph.D. degree.
Pre-Doctoral Internship	Paid	1 year, 20–40 hours per week	Pre-Ph.D., often 3rd, 4th, or 5th year	A formal work agreement with an external organization. Usually paid directly to the individual. Completed prior to obtaining doctorate.
External Assistantship	Paid	9–12 months, 10–20 hours per week	Pre-Ph.D., often 3rd, 4th, or 5th year	An assistantship arranged by the department with external organizations. Paid as an assistantship to the individual, organization pays the university.
Practicum	Both	3–12 months, 8–10 hours per week	Master's	A formal agreement with an external organization. Paid or volunteer. Completed as a requirement of obtaining a master's degree.
Consulting Center Project	Both	10–100 hours total	Graduate	Usually paid but could be unpaid. Engages in a consulting project handled through a departmental or university consulting center.
Faculty Project	Paid	10–100 hours total	Graduate or Undergraduate	Usually paid but could be unpaid. Assists a faculty member with a consulting project.
In-Class Exercise	Unpaid	Less than 20 hours total	Graduate or Undergraduate	Applied project assigned by faculty member as part of requirements of course. May involve a real outside organization, but typically involves a simulated organization.
Field Experience	Both	4 months, 8–10 hours per week	Undergraduate	Paid or unpaid, part-time work with external organization.

a These are intended to illustrate some of the typical labels and characteristics of different types of practical experience. There is substantial variation in labeling and characteristics across institutions.

We recommend having at least a semester, or preferably two or more semesters, of I-O coursework under your belt before seeking an internship. The knowledge from courses like Employee Selection and Quantitative Methods is critical to having an experience in which you can really add value with your I-O training.

The ideal timing for an internship depends on several factors like program type and course load. For master's students, many will take an internship in the summer between their first and second years of graduate school, so that they can fully focus on the job without course conflicts. Others may work fewer hours for a more extended time frame during their second year. On the other hand, Ph.D. students typically intern later in their studies. Waiting until after coursework and any qualifying exams are complete before engaging in an internship will make it easier to complete the final requirements of your program. Some may take summer internships before that point, but it is more common to spend those summers working on research projects, such as your thesis or dissertation.

Internships vary in time commitment, contract length, and compensation. All these factors should be weighted with your specific goals and needs in mind. Full-time internships for the summer are great for those that want to be fully immersed in a role, while part-time internships for a year or more can give you the opportunity to see projects through from start to finish and really make the role your own.

Timing aside, as for the details of actually looking for internships when you are ready to do so, be sure to use your network of contacts. At this point you have had a chance to impress faculty members in class though participation and project work, you have befriended more advanced students in your program who have gone on to work in applied jobs, and you have met professionals in various job types at meetings like SIOP conferences. This network can all help you find openings and secure informational interviews.

There are also so many resources online these days that you can come up with plenty of leads relatively quickly. Specifically, LinkedIn, SIOP's JobNet, and job search platforms are great starting points.

TEXTBOX 8.1 DDOVERSPIKE FACEBOOK JOB PAGE

Dennis Doverspike maintains a job page on Facebook, where you can find I-O related jobs and internships posted. Please feel free to join this page at: www.facebook.com/groups/ddoverspikejobpage.

Types of internships range from roles across the I and O sides. With an *internal internship* on a company's HR team, you might have exposure to a wider range of I-O solutions such as training, attitude surveys, and performance management. These internships would be great for someone who wants to work on their business acumen and get their feet wet in different areas. There are also *external internships* at consulting firms with a certain expertise, which can vary in specificity and specialty area. Consulting roles can give you a different form of variety in the sense of working with diverse clients and projects. There are also other types such as research-focused internships, which can be internal or external, but mainly focus on applying theory to available data with an emphasis on presenting at conferences and publishing in journals.

The best fit for you will depend on the match between the organization (type, size, expectations of interns, approach to development) and your interests and professional goals. Generally speaking, we think the most important factors for a good internship are: 1) working under or with someone with an I-O background, and 2) having some variety in the work itself so that your experience is not limited, and you avoid being relegated to clerical work.

PREPARING FOR AN INTERNSHIP

From the very beginning of your graduate program, there are certain things you can do to prepare for your future internship. One simple but important task would be to make sure you keep all your class notes and projects organized so that you can easily refer to them later if you need to brush up on a certain concept for a project, or if you are asked for writing samples in the application process.

Throughout your education, you should try to be involved in applied work in some capacity if you plan on seeking a competitive internship. This can take on a lot of forms and is not necessarily a huge time commitment. Most I-O programs either have ongoing consulting work through the department, have faculty who are actively involved in consulting and bring on students for assistance, or have a dedicated consulting center with the purpose of getting graduate students involved in applied projects. Take advantage of these opportunities, as getting varied experience will give you an idea of what a full-fledged internship would be like, build skills you will use in future roles, and help you figure out the type of work that makes you most excited and engaged.

Once you have identified and applied for some potential internship opportunities, you will likely be invited for interviews. We cannot emphasize enough the importance of carrying yourself with professionalism in an interview. A lot of candidates look the same on paper in terms of their educational background, but being prepared, well-spoken, and personable in an interview can make you stand out from the competition. We will not provide a long list of general interviewing tips, as you can find such advice in an endless array of online resources. However, a few things that stand out as important are coming prepared to talk about different areas such as technical knowledge (so review those class notes!), situations you have encountered (think back and list times when you have demonstrated competencies like leadership, so that you do not draw a blank when asked), and your own interests and passions (take some time to think about your goals and how they align with potential internship experiences). Be prepared to be asked to participate in a small work sample test, such as writing up a validation report based on output from a statistical program and then presenting the results to a group of managers.

SUCCESS IN YOUR INTERNSHIP

Proactive communication is extremely important to getting the most out of your internship. Before you start you should have a long conversation, maybe even several long conversations, about logistics such as the expectations for hours, flexibility in switching work days around, expectations for travel, on-site versus remote work, and dress code.

Whether you take on part- or full-time work is a decision for you to make, but sometimes part-time internships end up becoming full-time because of large work demands and an intern's reluctance to set boundaries. Or on the other hand, there may be opportunities to work a few extra hours to supplement your income that you would not know about unless you ask.

You can get ahead of these problems by verbalizing your priorities and time constraints, but also keep in mind that you should be flexible since applied work does not always neatly follow the office schedule. For example, being willing to check email on your days off or stay late when you are coming up on a deadline, will show that you are a team player, and will make it easy for the organization to reciprocate when you need to take days off to work on a dissertation draft or attend a conference.

One of the biggest errors students at all levels make is believing that the rest of the world follows an academic calendar. When universities take winter or summer breaks, capitalism does not suddenly grind to a halt. In many cases, organizations want to spend their consulting budget before the end of the year, which means working overtime between Thanksgiving and New Year's Day. External organizations will not always care if you have a big test coming up, work must get done and deadlines must be met.

You should be clear about the types of projects you want in an internship so that your employer can keep your interests in mind. Ask your direct supervisor their typical work style and discuss matters like whether they expect regular check-ins, whether they take a hands-on approach or leave interns to figure things out on their own, and whether they set strict internal deadlines or expect projects to just move along. Neither style is better or worse but knowing what to expect upfront will help you navigate this new environment.

TEXTBOX 8.2 INTERNSHIP EXPERIENCE REDUX

If you find yourself in an internship that fails to provide you with the types of experience that you want and should be receiving, instead of complaining, take initiative and pitch a new project idea to your supervisor. Be respectful when you do this and be prepared to sell the advantages to the organization of your proposal.

Internships require a level of independence and autonomy that you might not be used to if you have always been a full-time student. Although your supervisor is there to advise and guide you, realistically they may not have a lot of time for those activities. You may get assignments that are not as clearly defined as assignments in graduate school, and you may have to get creative with proposing solutions or potential avenues to pursue based on your training, creativity, and problem-solving skills.

Lastly, time management in an internship is something that cannot be emphasized enough. In graduate school, you might be able to get away with working right up until deadlines or even turning in assignments late, but in applied settings, your task is often one piece of a much larger project. You will find that maintaining organization in your work is a necessity and you will need to communicate regularly with your teammates so that they can anticipate if there will be delays in your ability to complete a project.

WHAT TO DO IF YOU GRADUATE WITHOUT AN INTERNSHIP

Finding and completing an internship in graduate school is strongly encouraged for graduate students that want to go into an applied career. Ultimately, a lot of students end up graduating without internship experience though, which could happen for many reasons. You might have been preparing for an academic career and changed your mind in your final months of graduate school. You might not have found a good fit or been able to make an internship work with your schedule, or you may never have gotten an offer. If you do end up in this or a similar situation when you reach graduation, do not worry because you can still land a great job.

It will come down to your ability to "sell" the applied experiences you have had in graduate school. Depending on your program and courses, you may have had applied projects in which you delivered a product to an organization, or closely simulated what that would be like with a hypothetical organization based on materials provided by your instructor. Whatever applied work you have done through a consulting center or a professor's practice will become more important: if you have been actively involved in consulting with a faculty member, you can show that you have similar experience as someone who did a formal internship. Talk to people about what they expect in candidates, and if you need it, take some time to round out your experience. This might mean helping a local non-profit with some survey work, or even taking an internship before applying to your first full-time job. Luckily, right now in I-O there are more jobs than organizations can fill, so think about how to best turn yourself into a desirable candidate.

THE DREADED ETERNAL A.B.D.

A continuing problem in I-O Psychology is that a significant number of students end up being "too successful" in their internship. It's a great thing to find you truly enjoy the work you do, and if you impress the organization, you may be offered and take a high-paying job before even coming close to finishing your degree. The result of all this internship success is that while you are engaged in compelling work, enjoying a comfortable income, and frequently traveling, less and less time is spent on the process of proposing or completing the dissertation. This leads to the all too common, never-ending, *All But Dissertation* or *A.B.D.* stage.

All Ph.D. programs wrestle with finding a solution to this dilemma, but the real answer comes down to the motivation and internal willpower of the *A.B.D.* student. The individual involved must keep their academic goals in mind and avoid the temptations of promotions that come with more time-consuming workloads. Once you start making money, it is tempting to engage in various pleasure-seeking activities, such as a vacation to Europe. Our advice is simply to avoid the temptation, work on that dissertation.

It is certainly possible to work a full-time job and still finish the dissertation. Successful students structure their activities and calendar, so that every day, or more likely nights and weekends, time is set aside to work on the dissertation. Of course, this is not easy, but it is the only way to avoid becoming a permanent *A.B.D.*

*****

There are all kinds of internships available for I-O graduate students. We recommend internship experience for everyone, but especially master's students and those that want to work in applied settings. Internships can be internal, external, or with another focus entirely. Some students do a different internship every summer, others stay in one organization for two years and get to know the business deeply. We see the keys to success in internships as 1) utilizing your network to see what options are out there, 2) working with other I-O practitioners who can bridge the gap between your academic studies and the workplace, and 3) getting varied experience in different areas of I-O and project types.

CHAPTER 9

Licensure and Certification

Licensure is a controversial topic in I-O Psychology and one that a lot of students do not receive enough information on from their program faculty. In this chapter, we will deal with topics related to licensure and certification. In particular, questions frequently asked by students about licensure will be addressed, including:

- Why the debate over licensure?
- Do you need licensure?
- How do you go about becoming licensed?
- What about other types of certification?

As an illustrative story for this chapter, in Table 9.1 we present an offering from Brodie Gregory Riordan. We find her tale appropriate for this chapter, as Brodie practices coaching and has obtained coaching certification.

THE LICENSURE DEBATE

Licensing is the granting of permission by some authority, in the United States it is usually a state or state board, to an individual to practice an occupation. Licensure is generally mandated by law. Psychology is a regulated profession in 64 jurisdictions in the United States and Canada. Thus, in almost all states in the United States, and in the Canadian provinces, an individual must be licensed as a psychologist to use the title "Psychologist" or "I-O Psychologist."

In most states licensure is generic, which means that it applies to all psychologists and specialties are not identified nor specified. Licensure is

Table 9.1 Brodie Gregory Riordan, Ph.D., What If I Had Missed That Lecture?

It is a clear, sunny April morning in 2002. I walk down the beautiful, historic Colonnade at Washington and Lee University, headed to a guest lecture from a 1984 alumnus, Paul Levy, entitled "I-O, I-O, it's off to work I go." I am a psychology major with little to no sense of what I should do with my life, and vague familiarity with the field of I-O Psychology. I also debated staying in bed and skipping this lecture.

And what if I had? Many times, I have asked myself, what on earth would I be doing now if I had skipped that lecture? During that lecture the lightbulb finally came on and I realized what I wanted to do with my life.

I had always loved psychology but was not excited by a career in counseling or clinical. This idea of using psychology to get the right people into the right jobs and to grow, develop, and help them reach their potential, all informed by science, spoke to me. People spend so much time at work, and therefore should be doing things that they enjoy, that are a good fit for their skills, and that work can be an incredible vehicle to actually improve people's lives, skills, and abilities.

Two years later, I started at The University of Akron to study I-O Psychology with Paul Levy as my advisor. In my first few days of grad school it became clear to me that Paul focused a lot of his research on feedback. I thought to myself, "How oddly specific. And how boring!" But it was only a matter of time until I, too, became a feedback zealot, with a deep interest in coaching, leadership development, and the critical role of feedback in both.

During my time at The University of Akron, my mission was to take advantage of every opportunity and prepare myself for any I-O career path. I taught undergrad classes nearly every semester, always had at least one research project going, and did several internships and contract gigs with consulting firms and within organizations. I could see myself pursing the academic, applied internal, and external consulting paths and wanted to be sure I had the experiences necessary to pursue them all, just in case. Now, roughly ten years out of grad school, I've done all three.

My first "real job" out of graduate school was an internal role at Procter and Gamble (P&G), where I worked in Global Leadership Development and had big opportunities leading our coaching work and performance management process, among other things. I learned at an exponential rate at P&G and discovered how much I love visiting manufacturing sites.

An unusual opportunity lured me away from P&G and into a brief stint in academia. One of my former professors at Washington and Lee University was going on sabbatical, and what better opportunity to try out I-O Psychology in the department than with a visiting professor? I spent one glorious year teaching alongside my undergraduate professors at my alma mater, with flexibility to teach not only I-O and social psychology classes, but also seminars in my passion areas, including leadership and peak performance.

The beauty of a temporary role is that you do not have to be sneaky when searching for your next opportunity. Three days after the end of the academic year at Washington and Lee, I started that next opportunity in external consulting with PDRI; six months into my tenure we were acquired by CEB, and I had the unique experience of going through an acquisition.

At PDRI, I was thrilled to work for an I-O "Original Gangster," where I would continue this red thread of leadership development, coaching, feedback, and helping people unlock their potential. At PDRI, I worked with private and public sector clients and was afforded autonomy and independence to develop client relationships and pursue work that truly interested me.

My interest in coaching and feedback grew. Paul Levy and I had the opportunity to write a book about using feedback in consulting, which opened the door to more feedback-focused client work. My coaching work also evolved. Where I had previously designed and managed coaching programs and strategy, now I was actually doing the coaching.

I figured I should legitimize my coaching practice, and enrolled in Georgetown's leadership coach training program. I foolishly assumed I already knew so much about coaching and was doing the training simply to check a box and get certified, but soon realized that I knew very little and my practice was subpar.

My approach to coaching was limited by my I-O Psychology lens. I came to the program with a strong foundation in empirical research on coaching, motivation, feedback, goal setting, and leadership development. But coaching is multidisciplinary, something that I did not understand or appreciate. I discovered blind spots in my ability to *really* listen, to be truly non-directive and flow with, rather than control, the conversation, to pick up on emotions and body language. I had focused disproportionately on the rational, on what's being said, rather than the emotional and what's not being said.

Rigorous coach training programs include not only hours and hours of coaching practice, but also hours and hours of being coached. One of the risks of working with a coach is the unavoidable surfacing of how you really feel, what you really want, and what is getting in the way. In addition to developing my coaching skills during my training, I experienced transformative personal development, which ultimately led me to make another transition in my career.

The lifestyle challenges, travel, and billable time of consulting were wearing on me and I was inspired to redouble my focus on leadership development and potential. An internal role in learning and leadership development for partners at McKinsey and Company was the right next move for me. I joined McKinsey in 2016 and have enjoyed opportunities perfectly aligned to my interests: coaching (both as a coach and programmatic work), building feedback best practices and a forward-looking perspective into review processes, and developing programming that helps people develop their dialogue and listening skills, clarify their priorities and aspirations, and achieve their full potential through work.

Over the years I have received a surprising degree of criticism for the "non-linear" nature of my career path. To me, I was always doing the same kind of work, and developing my knowledge and skills, just in different contexts. My passion for helping people unlock their potential, for coaching, feedback, and leadership development have always been at the forefront. My combined experiences at Procter and Gamble (internal), Washington and Lee (academia), and PDRI/CEB (external/consulting) prepared me for the role at McKinsey (internal in a consulting firm). I look forward to making another career choice that may seem surprising or unusual to others, but continues to take me on this journey *to help people reach their full potential* through work.

People often tell me that they can see how much I love my occupation. I agree – I feel energized and excited when I talk about I-O psychology and cannot imagine what I would be doing if I had not discovered the field. Thank goodness I went to Paul's guest lecture back in 2002.

so common, that in Table 9.2, it is easier to list the states that do not have a generic licensure law, the jurisdictions that only license health service psychologists, and the states that exempt general applied psychologists, rather than list the states requiring licensure.

So, bottom line, if you want to call yourself a "Psychologist.," you need to be licensed. However, surveys suggest that 10% or less of I-O Psychologists are licensed, and that number continues to drop for recent graduates. Compare this to other fields like Consulting Psychology where approximately 50% or more of all Ph.D.s are licensed, and you will start to see the issues around the debate. Unlicensed I-O Psychologists refer to themselves using a number of labels or titles such as management consultant, human resource consultant, organizational development specialist, and assessment specialist (refer back to Table 2.1). There are also those individuals who are exempted from licensure laws, such as those working for the U.S. federal government, and academics serving as professors of psychology.

From the perspective of someone new to the field, you might wonder why the debate or controversy? Why the resistance of I-O Psychologists to complying with licensure requirements? Basically, it starts with the need to differentiate the two types of psychologists, those involved in health care, such as clinical and counseling psychologists, and those who are categorized as general applied psychologists, including consulting and I-O Psychologists.

Table 9.2 States with Exceptions to a General, Generic License

U.S. jurisdictions that do not have a generic licensure law for psychologists

- Colorado
- District of Columbia
- Hawaii
- Illinois
- New Mexico
- Utah

U.S. jurisdictions that restrict licensure or only license Health Service Psychologists (HSPs)

- Georgia (has separate license for I-O)
- Hawaii (I-O Psychologists must register)
- Illinois
- New Mexico
- Utah

U.S. jurisdictions that exempt General Applied Psychologists and I-O Psychologists from licensure

- Hawaii
- Illinois
- North Carolina
- South Dakota
- Wyoming

Laws which have been developed to apply to psychologists in health care, are often seen as lacking in applicability to I-O Psychologists who work in completely different capacities. In addition, I-O Psychologists often argue that the public they serve is not in danger of being harmed, and, therefore, the main objectives of licensing laws, which is to protect the public, does not apply to the work performed by I-O Psychologists.

DO YOU NEED TO BE LICENSED?

To answer the question simply, no, you do not have to be licensed. You may not be able to call yourself an "I-O Psychologist" as your title, but as do most other I-O professionals, you can refer to yourself by a number of other titles and indicate that you received a degree in I-O Psychology. However, there are several reasons why you might want to be licensed, including:

- Being able to call yourself, refer to yourself, and advertise yourself as a psychologist.
- As a way of increasing your credibility with clients, the public, and the courts.
- Establishing a legal basis for claiming confidentiality in your dealings with clients.

Our view is that you should at least consider the possibility of licensure, become knowledgeable about licensure, keep your options open as much as possible during graduate school, and when the time comes make an informed, knowledgeable decision as to whether you need to, or want to, seek licensure.

BECOMING LICENSED AS A PSYCHOLOGIST

The route to licensure is a long one, and if you are considering going down this path, you should start preparing and documenting your own history of training and experience as soon as you start graduate school. Typical requirements for licensure include:

- A Ph.D. or similar doctoral degree from a psychology training program that includes residency and supervised professional experience and/or internship (in some cases the program must be accredited by the American Psychological Association.)
- Courses demonstrating competence in core areas of psychology.
- 2000–3000 hours of supervised experience.
- Taking and passing the Examination for Professional Practice in Psychology (EPPP), although soon there may be the requirement that both the EPPP1 and EPPP2 be passed.
- Taking and passing any state specific jurisprudence or oral examinations.

The EPPP is a licensing examination developed by the Association of State and Provincial Psychology Boards (ASPPB). Currently, students complete a version that will soon be known as the EPPP1; this exam is given online and is designed to include content from all areas of psychology. Additionally, a new exam, the EPPP2, may soon serve as an additional hurdle for those seeking licensure.

The national exams are given online and are designed to be "generic" tests that include items from many fields of psychology. A question that we frequently are asked by students is whether particular I-O programs have APA accreditation. Unknowingly, the student is asking a trick question. The APA only accredits programs in clinical, counseling, and school psychology; there is no accreditation for I-O programs. Therefore, graduates of I-O programs must individually document and defend the adequacy of their graduate education.

OTHER TYPES OF CERTIFICATION

Beyond licensure, there are other options for professional recognition. Depending upon one's specialty area and interests, various types of certification are available. Technically, certification refers to a recognition that an individual has voluntarily met some requirement set by an organization.

For those wishing to specialize in human resources, the Society for Human Resource Management (SHRM) offers very popular certification options. The SHRM Certified Professional (SHRM-CP®) is designed for early- and mid-career professionals, and the SHRM Senior Certified Professional (SHRM-SCP®) is intended for senior-level practitioners. Further information on the certificates and the associated examinations can be found at the SHRM website.

For practitioners working in the public sector, The International Public Management Association for Human Resources (IPMA-HR) provides opportunities to be certified as either a IPMA-CP or an IPMA-SCP. Further information can be found at the IPMA-HR website.

If you are interested in marketing yourself as an executive or leadership coach, a variety of organizations offer coaching certifications. One of the best known is that offered by the International Coaching Federation, or ICF. Again, which offers certification at a number of experience levels including Associate Certified Coach, Professional Certified Coach, and Master Certified Coach. In Table 9.1, Brodie Gregory Riordan discusses her pursuit of coaching certification.

In medicine, a physician can obtain board certification in order to establish exceptional expertise in a particular specialty. Psychologists can also obtain board certification in order to demonstrate having obtained a high level of proficiency in a specialty area.

For psychologists, one of the best-known board certifications is that offered by the American Board of Professional Psychology or ABPP. When you see ABPP after a psychologist's name, they have obtained board certification in some specialty, which means they have gone beyond the requirements of licensure and has achieved exceptional expertise, meeting a "gold standard." ABPP has been certifying I-O Psychology specialists for over 50 years. For I-O Psychologists, the relevant specialty board is the American Board of Organizational and Business Consulting Psychology Board (ABOBCP). To apply, you must have a psychology license and two years of post-licensure experience.

*****

We hope to have given you an understanding of the issues around licensing and certification in I-O Psychology. If you have no interest in becoming licensed, you will be just fine functioning as a professional with an I-O Psychology degree. But, a few people do seek licensure for reasons like maintaining the identity of a psychologist. If this appeals to you, you should start planning and organizing relevant documentation early in graduate school, as it is a long process and programs are not designed to have you meet all the requirements. You will want to make sure that you take the courses that will qualify you to sit for licensure. In addition, you should make sure any practical work is conducted under the supervision of a licensed psychologist. Other certifications can be a great addition to your practice depending on your specialty area and we encourage you to explore those options.

CHAPTER 10

Cha-Cha-Changes

Transitioning into I-O

Changes and transitions are a part of growth, a part of living. As psychologists, one would think we would be more attuned to the need of some individuals to make career changes. The truth is that most students we are familiar with take a traditional career route; they apply to graduate programs either as an undergraduate student or after a year of work or research experience, enter graduate school within a year or two of completing an undergraduate program, and attend traditional, brick-and-mortar universities. The applications and criteria for most programs are set up to reflect this traditional orientation.

Times are changing though, and many individuals may not decide to pursue I-O Psychology right out of college. There are those individuals who start, or even complete, a Ph.D. program in clinical or counseling psychology, and then try working in an organizational setting, finding that applying psychology to work problems is where their true passion lies. Other individuals may be working as an executive nearing retirement at a major firm and decide that they want to teach or become an academic. Or, someone may be working in a totally different field for a terrible organization or a bad boss and say to themselves, "This organization needs changing, I want to learn about what can be done, how do I become an I-O Psychologist?"

This chapter was written for those individuals who would like to make a career change or move. We have chosen to concentrate on three types of transitions:

1. The terminal master's recipient who decides to pursue a Ph.D. in I O Psychology.
2. The individual with a Ph.D. in a different specialty who would like to move into I-O Psychology, either full-time or as an additional component to their practice.

3. The non-psychologist who wants to make a complete career change into I-O Psychology, though many of these individuals end up in related occupation such as human resources.

The following career story is a decidedly different one, coming from an individual, Ernest Hoffman, who's experience as a minister gave him a unique perspective in his next pursuit of becoming an I-O Psychologist. We hope you enjoy reading his story in Table 10.1 below.

Table 10.1 Ernest Hoffman, Ph.D., An Unconventional Path from Minister to I-O Psychologist

As a senior psychology major, I was faced with a difficult choice. Serving as a spiritual leader had long been a dream of mine, but I was also intrigued by the prospect of impacting people and organizations as an I-O Psychologist. Most of my friends and colleagues advised that it would make the most sense to live a long, fulfilling career in I-O Psychology before doing ministry in my later years, if not my retirement. So naturally, I chose to go in the opposite direction, but I did it for a very intentional reason. I felt that *doing* leadership and being "in the trenches" for a few years would be a great precursor for *studying* leadership or consulting with leaders in a business setting.

Confident in my choice, I started work on my Master of Divinity degree at a mainline denominational seminary within months of completing my bachelor's degree. Shortly after turning 26, I was called to serve a faith community with approximately 400 members near Detroit, Michigan, where I remained for nearly four years. The leadership experiences and challenges I faced during those years were things I could have never anticipated from the classroom. Managing people who were two and three times my age, attempting to influence volunteers when they neither formally reported to me nor received a paycheck, confronting residual dysfunctionality that had been left behind by predecessors, and remaining sufficiently connected yet sufficiently differentiated as a leader were just some of the things I had never thought about in my undergraduate courses. Throughout my time in ministry, I frequently returned to my notes from psychology classes with two questions that would eventually send me back to graduate school: (1) what can I learn and apply to this context from I-O Psychology, and (2) what can I create within both of these fields from the place of my unique experiences?

I was nervous but determined in the Fall of 2009 as I took the Graduate Record Exam and started filling out applications for a number of excellent programs. Fear of rejection or missed opportunity loomed large, but I was even more concerned about my ability to succeed as a non-traditional student in a top-tier program. By the time I started my first day as an M.A./Ph.D. student in July of 2010, I had been out of school for four years and out of a university setting for just over eight years. The investment that my program faculty and advisor chose to make in me was not lost on me, nor was my choice to leave full-time ministry and homework-free evenings to return to school. I was determined to prove to everyone that this was a great decision, largely in hopes of paving the way for future individuals who might want to follow in a similar path. At the front of my mind was this vision of my faculty talking through a future set of program applications, pulling out the profile of a promising 30-something, and remembering the last time they took a chance on someone like that.

One of this book's co-authors administered my first exam, and I will never forget how long the 20-foot walk from my office to his seemed to be when it was time for him to give me feedback and a grade for my performance. Did I make the right choice? Would I be calling my denominational office in an hour to see what positions were available? The feedback I received in that conversation was so affirming and supportive that it kept me going through many challenges to follow. It would mark the beginning of a successful journey through graduate school, where I felt like my experiences as a leader gave me so much insight to add as we reviewed articles, worked on research projects with faculty, consulted with organizations, and proposed and executed independent research projects. I found and embraced a surprising identity for myself as a boundary-spanner, someone capable of bridging the best of what two different disciplines have to offer so that everyone could benefit. It started with connecting spiritual leadership with organizational leadership, and then I started branching out into other areas of psychology, marketing, and even quantum physics.

These diverse experiences prepared me to accept a position as a management consultant about four years ago. In my current role, I wear a lot of hats that include assessment writing, coaching, leadership development, data analysis, and owning our company's research function. The ability to draw from my experiences as a minister has been critical to connecting with leaders who are new to their careers and facing challenges like the ones I encountered. Beyond that, I found the courage to challenge individuals to venture off their own beaten paths and try directions that were unconventional. I often joke with my facilitation groups that I could have saved six years of studying leadership by realizing that leadership really amounts to a single word, whether you are a minister or an I-O Psychologist. Leadership is *influence*, plain and simple. I would like to think that my story will someday influence another person to take a route less-travelled, even if it happens to be the person who is holding this book.

Choosing this path was the best choice I ever made. It gave me so much courage to do the unconventional beyond my days in graduate school. It proved that I could chart my own course – creating things that may have never existed were it not for more than one person who was willing to take a chance on something and someone that was a little out of the ordinary.

TERMINAL MASTER'S

The terminal master's in I-O is an excellent choice as a degree option and there are many extremely successful individuals who have stopped their education at the master's degree level. A few of our most famous and most influential I-O Psychologists have master's degrees. However, some individuals graduate with a master's degree and find that there remains a nagging feeling, a fire burning in the belly, which says "you really want to be Dr. so-and-so," or maybe their parents just always wanted a doctor in the family. Some master's degree recipients go out on the job market and have trouble finding a good fit for them, and realize that by going back to school for the Ph.D. they will have a wider variety of job options and the opportunity to start at more senior levels and with higher salaries.

Our advice is that you should make sure you have a true deep desire for the Ph.D. if you are going to go back to school after working for a few years with your master's. If you found yourself at the top of your class in your master's program, you might like the challenge of returning to the academic environment. Even so, going back to school can be very tough. If you're out in the real world, you may be enjoying the full-time salary, your free time on weekends, and prioritizing your family. Going back for the Ph.D. requires making sacrifices in every area. However, if you really need that Ph.D., then go for it; it is not easy, but it can be done.

Unfortunately, our experience has been that many traditional programs prefer students right out of college and may not even consider those with a master's. Be sure to check with the programs you are considering to make sure they take individuals who already have a master's and work experience. Talk with faculty about how they would adjust the typical program structure and timeline for someone in your position: *Would you need to retake courses you've already completed? Would your master's thesis from your previous institution fulfill the requirement in the other program?* Admissions committees may not be totally familiar with such cases, but a willingness to work with you is a good sign. In terms of potential program types, you should consider online programs, especially if you intend to continue working.

As we will repeat in this chapter, the personal statement letter will be critical for you. You need to make the case that you are 1) serious about seeking the Ph.D., 2) truly committed and aware of the sacrifices, and 3) have a workable plan for managing the career and life issues that will arise.

SWITCHING SPECIALTIES

One of the more popular workshops we have given at state psychological conferences is on transitioning into I-O work from Clinical or Counseling Psychology. This can involve adding to one's suite of interventions but remaining primarily a health care professional, or a complete change in specialty. Some changes may be more seamless; for example, the family therapist who moves into working with teams or family businesses, the police psychologist who offers pre- and post-offer assessments, or the counseling psychologist who becomes a coach. Recent years have seen more and more professionals making the choice to switch from therapy with patients to coaching with executives and managers.

For psychologists interested in a transition, there are a number of options. One popular choice recently has been to seek out training leading to business coaching certification. Other types of training and certification may be acquired as well, for example administering and interpreting specific types of tests such as the MMPI with police and safety personnel. Another option is to seek post-doctoral training with a traditional or online Ph.D. program. You should contact the programs you might be interested in to see if post-doctoral training is a possibility.

Of course, any type of change in specialty designation involves ethical issues. In particular, Section 2 of the *American Psychological Association Ethical Principles of Psychologists and Code of Conduct* (2017) deals with the topic of "Competence." Specifically, the *Ethics Code* states that psychologists who act in an ethical manner provide services only within their competence. In addition, we have come across some ethical problems involving psychologists trying to act as both a mental health–oriented therapist and business coach to the same clients, leading to dual relationship conflicts.

NON-PSYCHOLOGIST TO PSYCHOLOGIST

The third type of change we discuss is the most complex, the transition from the non-psychologist to psychologist. There could be many reasons for this decision: some might spend 20 years working at a job they really dislike, and decide to pursue I-O to learn how to fix the problems they experienced like poor leadership and ineffective communication. Others might already have work experience in consulting or human resources and realize that an I-O Psychology degree will open doors for seniority and different types of work. The common element is that it is a major career shift. As with our other career shifters, those transitioning to I-O Psychology are making an investment in their long-term career that requires giving up seniority, income, and free time in the short-term.

This is probably the trickiest shift to navigate, in that the individual may or may not have a psychology undergraduate degree or the necessary prerequisites to seek an advanced I-O Psychology degree. So, the first step would be to either identify programs that have more lenient minimum requirements, or to go back to an undergraduate institution part-time to complete the necessary psychology courses required as prerequisites. This preliminary work could be completed at a local college or through an online option. With the necessary courses completed, we refer you back to Chapter 4 to think about the other components of the application. Ideally, it would be great to get some research experience by working in a professor's lab for a few months before applying to graduate school. If this is not an option for you, we encourage you to get creative with the resources in your job to work on I-O related projects that could be considered research or draw on the same skills like data analysis.

Going back to school for a traditional M.A. or Ph.D. in I-O Psychology after working in another field will be tough, but we have seen that success is possible and we encourage you to pursue it if you think it is right for you. Some individuals switching from non-psychology areas will probably find an online option to be attractive. For executives, there are executive M.B.A. programs and now even a number of executive D.B.A. or Ph.D. programs. Such educational options can be expensive but may appeal to executives looking to eventually return to the classroom as an academic or professor. This option could be attractive for an executive who is facing retirement and has always dreamt of sharing their wisdom with young people in a college or university, and realizes later in life that a Ph.D. is needed to pursue this vision. Or, it might be an employee of a large organization who is fed up with organizational inefficiencies and wants to dedicate themselves to the research that could solve such problems.

*****

As psychologists, we should encourage individuals to follow their dreams: those that have attained a master's degree and want to pursue a Ph.D., those switching specialties in psychology, and non-psychologists making a career change to I-O are in for a challenging endeavor, but one that will be worthwhile to find an occupation where they fit and that makes them happy. In the future, we hope more programs recognize the importance of easing transitions and offering retraining. As noted, the personal statement letter will be critical for those transitioning, as an opportunity to make a strong case for your fit to your identified programs. Whatever your path, know that in this field there is sure to be someone with a similar story, with determination and the right guidance you can definitely achieve your goals.

PART 4

CAREERS

CHAPTER 11

Academic Jobs and Careers

There are a lot of driving forces for those that decide to pursue academic careers. Maybe you have always wanted an opportunity to teach others and shape young minds, or to conduct impactful research. Maybe you have watched one too many movies about college life and have always dreamed about living in an ivory tower dressed in a tweed jacket with elbow patches. Or, more likely, your professors or advisors in your graduate career encouraged you (though a cynic might argue they brainwashed you) into carrying on their legacy by pursuing a career in academia. Maybe you are still undecided as to what you want to do with your life, and are going to apply to academic, consulting, industry, and public-sector jobs.

Be forewarned, there is a reason that those in academe often speak of the external world as "the real world," as if academics inhabit a fantasy realm akin to Hogwarts School of Witchcraft and Wizardry. Well, at graduation time, we do all wear funny long robes. And on the day you obtain your master's or doctorate degree, you will receive you own fine robe with fancy velvet patches while your advisor and others hood you in your own colorful cape. The world of academics often plays according to its own rules and timelines. In response, this chapter covers the topic of applying for academic jobs and what to expect if you do decide to pursue a career as a professor. Areas to be covered in this chapter include:

- What are your options?
- When and how to apply.
- The application process.
- The academic interview process.
- Your first days, years, and beyond.

In Table 11.1, Alexandra I. Zelin discusses the positives and negatives of being a new, young professor in a terminal master's program. We have also included brief insights from two other academics later on in this chapter for your reading pleasure.

Table 11.1 Alexandra I. Zelin, Ph.D., A Career in Academia

When beginning my job search in academia I knew that I wanted a job in a teaching-focused school and was not necessarily picky about whether it had a master's program in I-O Psychology. I also knew that I wanted to be able to continue my research program, just not at the publish-or-perish level. Luckily, during my job search year, there was a great mix of schools at the undergraduate and master's level looking to hire an assistant professor. One of the early realizations I had was that working in a master's program meant that I was not the sole I-O within a psychology department, or even within an entire college/university. The potential for collaborations and discussions about the field itself on a daily basis with other I-O faculty members became incredibly appealing. When offered a position at the University of Tennessee at Chattanooga, a department with a strong I-O master's program, I jumped at the chance. The fit felt right and I could see myself in the city long-term!

Because I attended an undergraduate university without graduate students on the main campus (teaching-focused), followed by a graduate university with a high number of Ph.D. programs (research-focused), I thought I was prepared to be working somewhere in the middle of those two. In some ways I was right, and in some ways, I learned a whole lot more. I knew starting out that I would need to balance my teaching and research responsibilities, but I did not know just how much focus was placed on each of them: you are expected to teach at a level of someone not expected to complete numerous research projects, but also research at a level of someone not expected to have a high teaching load. The feeling of being pulled in numerous directions and not knowing what to focus on was overwhelming at first (and sometimes still is). Having great mentors who will help "protect" you and guide you into/away from needed career moves and knowing which projects to accept and which to pass, are crucial.

I also learned that the feeling of imposter syndrome is real – walking in to teach a graduate class knowing that I was expected to be the expert was disconcerting. Graduate students ask more in-depth questions than undergraduate students, so these classes are much more cognitively challenging than teaching an undergraduate course. As most master's students will graduate into the workforce, many class questions relate to the direct translation of theory into practice. It is hard when asked "have you ever seen . . .?" and you do not have any consulting experience within that area. I learned that throwing the question out to the class was helpful because sometimes a fellow student has an answer based on a previous experience in their own jobs. Additionally, because master's courses are much more applied-focused than doctoral courses, practice in applying theory is imperative. It is a necessity to develop applied exercises for the class to complete, as just focusing on theory will not help students directly apply it in their internships or on day one of their jobs. The applied focus also means finding different textbooks than those used in my own graduate classes; textbooks which are more applied and give real-world examples rather than just summarizing literature are important.

The applied vs. research distinction in course content made, I realized that I wished I had taken advantage of more consulting opportunities in graduate school to broaden my applied experience base. If you are thinking about teaching in a master's program, I recommend taking as many consulting opportunities as you can, because having the applied experience will help immensely when describing how to translate the research/textbook readings into applied work. I also recommend ensuring you take on applied projects as a professor as well, so you are current with the business trends and can translate your experiences into valuable class lessons. I foresee this being a challenge in balancing responsibilities for myself, especially because of the strong teaching-research expectations at master's level institutions.

Last, try to have as many research articles "in progress" and as much written up as you can before you start the fall semester of your first year. I have learned that many of the articles published during your probationary period are those you worked on in graduate school (at least the first two to three years) as the publishing process is incredibly long. You also do not accomplish as much in your first year as you would like . . .

With that said, I love that my job allows me to engage in high levels of both teaching and research without having to sacrifice either one, and I would not have it any other way!

WHAT ARE YOUR OPTIONS?

Hopefully, you have made yourself an attractive applicant for academic employment by being successful in graduate school (see Chapter 7). Specifically, you would want to have:

- Made steady and reasonable progress throughout graduate school.
- Taught classes and received favorable ratings as a teacher.
- Engaged in research including conference presentations and published work.

- Obtained practical experience.
- Impressed your professors, such that they are willing to write you recommendation letters.

The typical professorship is a tenure-track position, in which you are hired at the assistant professor level with the potential to earn tenure after a certain period. Although not all faculty positions offer the possibility of tenure, obtaining a tenure-track position is highly prized. What exactly is tenure, and why is it so highly valued? Tenure is unique to the teaching profession and refers to the "granting of lifetime employment as an academic, where the person can be terminated only under extreme or unusual circumstances." Earning tenure is associated with academic freedom, referring to the "freedom to teach, write, and publish opinions and facts without being subject to administrative review and with freedom from retaliation or repercussions." The granting of tenure represents a potentially very lengthy commitment on the part of the university, which is one of the reasons some institutions are moving away from tenure. Recently, more and more institutions are moving to larger numbers of adjunct, part-time, and non-tenured faculty; somewhat confusingly, non-tenured faculty are often referred to as "clinical professors" or a "professor of practice."

As you know, most jobs in academe involve teaching, but being a professor usually encompasses much more than that. At most colleges and universities, in order to gain tenure and promotions in rank, the faculty member is subject to an evaluation of composed of teaching ratings, service provided to the community and institution (such as in the form of committee membership), and contributions to the scholarly community in the form of published original works of research. Different institutions and program types weigh these three aspects of professorship differently: some programs are very research-focused and have high expectations for publishing one's research to earn tenure (i.e., the dreaded juggernaut of publish-or-perish), while others emphasize the teaching and service components more highly.

TEXTBOX 11.1 A BRIEF THOUGHT ON ACADEME FROM JOAN DAVISON

The professoriate is not an occupation. Do not enter a life in academics if your goal is to obtain fame or fortune, for there is no guarantee that you will reach such a lofty objective. Serving as a professor is a vocation. A professor's legacy is carried and spread by his or her students.

Similar to your decision when applying to graduate school, you will need to make a choice as to what program type is best suited to you as an I-O Psychology professor. One way to think about it is that there are different expectations as function of the highest degree awarded by the department. If the department only produces bachelor's degrees, the professor might be expected to publish a few book chapters or journal articles, with a higher emphasis on teaching, mentoring undergraduate students, and service. For master's degree departments, research expectations could be one journal article per year, with teaching opportunities at both undergraduate and master's levels, and mentoring or advising both undergraduate and master's students. For Ph.D. granting departments, an assistant professor might be expected to publish one article per year in a top journal in the field, teach graduate and undergraduate courses, and advise graduate students on master's theses and doctoral dissertations.

Another distinction is whether to go into a Psychology or Business department, which both have advantages and drawbacks. For those who are highly attached to Psychology as a part of their professional identity, looking for a position in a Psychology department would be a clear choice. On the other hand, Business departments offer more opportunities for collaboration across disciplines. While business schools tend to have more resources and may offer higher salaries, the culture among business school students is usually very different than among psychology students. Business schools tend to have a more applied focus, so you may have trouble collaborating with students and faculty that aren't sold on the value of I-O Psychology. Of course, some people might like the challenge of learning business acumen and translating the discipline to fit the wider organizational context.

TEXTBOX 11.2 ROSANNA MIGUEL ON THE VALUE OF I-O IN A BUSINESS SCHOOL

I discovered my life's work in a small, Jesuit business school, with class sizes averaging 30 students. Initially, I contemplated whether my I-O Psychology background would fit in a 'business' culture. I soon learned that business itself isn't a culture. It's about the people, their values and the school's mission. I crafted my role and found opportunities to add value by infusing I-O Psychology's strong measurement focus into my classes, emphasizing validity and reliability, data analysis, and metrics. My continued learning and student contributions have taught me that the field of I-O Psychology and Management & Human Resources complement one another well. This knowledge allows me to satisfy my greatest passion – having a profound impact on my students.

WHEN AND HOW TO APPLY

Time does become stretched in academe, and nowhere is this clearer than when applying for a traditional academic position. Initial interviews may take place more than a year before the job is to be filled; not exactly a quick or compact process. That means you should be prepared to apply more than a year in advance. So, for example if I wanted an academic job in the fall of 2021, I should be starting the application process in the spring of 2020, about a year and a half in advance of stepping into the classroom for my first day. This is especially true if you are considering applying for a traditional business school position. Many times, business schools will conduct initial interviews at the Academy of Management conference more than a year in advance. The Academy of Management usually meets in July or August, so the interviews held there are not for the upcoming fall semester, but for positions starting the next fall.

The actions of business schools have led to many psychology departments moving up their application and interviewing windows. As a result, psychology departments may schedule interviews as early as September or October of the fall semester, almost one year before the intended start date. The unintended consequence is that job postings appearing in the spring of the year are often not for hiring for the fall of the same year, but for positions where the individual will be starting a year and a half after the job is first posted. If you have guessed that the process in the other areas such as industry, consulting, and the public sector is much quicker, you are catching on to some of the unique aspects of the academic world.

Before you can apply, you must find job openings. At one time, a time which to many of you will seem like the dark ages, most I-O jobs in academe were posted in the *American Psychologist Monitor*, which was published monthly. Today, most university jobs will be found at either the SIOP jobs webpage or the Academy of Management jobs page. There you can search for jobs by type, location, and other attributes. You can also use employment related search engines, such as Indeed, to find academic jobs and have regular updates on opening sent to you. The use of employment related search engines is especially important if you are looking for online, remote, or adjunct positions.

In addition to searching these pages, we would recommend that if you are interested in working at a highly specific institution, such as your old undergraduate college or schools in the New York City area, you should identify your schools of interest and regularly check each school's employment webpage. Especially for smaller schools, new positions may never be posted to the major sites such as the SIOP or the Academy of Management websites. If your interest is in teaching for an online university, again you should consider searching each school's employment website. When you do so, you will usually be asked whether you want to receive regular emails of new openings, to which you should reply in the affirmative. There are also specialized employment related search engines that only look for those jobs that are considered telecommuting, online, or remote.

THE APPLICATION PROCESS

At this point you have located some positions or jobs of interest and are ready to apply. Today, the application process is usually completed online, although some schools may still request that materials be emailed or physically mailed to the head of the search committee for the position. Completing the online process will involve filling out a lengthy application, and then uploading or submitting a cover letter, curriculum vitae, and professional references. Some applications may request supplemental materials like past teaching evaluations, a statement of your teaching philosophy, or a statement of your research plans and interests.

In completing the online application form, you should be prepared to enter a great deal of information on your past and current life. At some point in the online application system, you will be asked to submit a cover letter. Our advice would be to prepare a generic cover letter, but then to modify the cover letter to fit the requirements of the specific position of interest. For the newly minted Ph.D., this letter will be approximately one to two pages and include the following paragraphs (For an example see Table 11.2):

cover letter

1. Formal indication of interest and application for the position. A brief statement of why you are qualified for the position.
2. Review of your educational background, including expected date of completion of degree if it is still in progress.
3. Review of your research experience and interests.
4. Discussion of your teaching experience and philosophy.
5. Thank you to the hiring committee.

In the normal world, you would next submit your résumé, in the world of academics you will instead submit an extensive document referred to as a "curriculum vitae" or just a "vita." For a senior faculty member, a vita may run 50 pages. For someone applying for the first academic job, the vita will typically be in the two to five-page range. Table 11.3 provides an outline of the sections contained in a typical vita.

Cover Letter Example

Table 11.2 Academic Cover Letter

Margaret Follies
Psychology Department
University of Stow
Stow, OH 44,224
mfollies@ustow.edu
10/5/2018

I would like to officially apply for the full-time, tenure track Faculty position in the Online Industrial-Organizational Psychology M.S. Program, in the Department of Psychology at the University of Kent. Currently, I am a graduate student in my final year completing my Ph.D. in Industrial-Organizational Psychology at the University of Stow. I will have my dissertation completed in the Summer of 2019. Attached you will find this cover letter and my vita. I would be happy to provide you and your committee with copies of any of my publications.

As mentioned above, I will have my doctorate in the field of Industrial-Organizational Psychology by the start date for your position, which would be the Fall of 2019. I am currently in the data collection phase of my dissertation under Dr. Lou D. Speaker on the topic of organizational persuasion policies. I consider myself an Organizational Psychologist with broad interests in persuasion, group dynamics, and diversity issues.

In terms of research productivity, I have started an active research program under Dr. Speaker on the topic of persuasion which I hope to continue. At this early point in my career, I have one major publication in *Personnel Assessment and Decisions*, one minor publication, and three manuscripts under review. One of the manuscripts under review is based on my thesis. I have presented research at three conferences so far and I am preparing several submissions for upcoming conferences.

I have two years of teaching experience, including having taught Introduction to Psychology as a teaching assistant. I also had complete responsibility for a course in Social Science Statistics, which I taught as an instructor at the local community college. My teaching ratings are consistently in the 3.3 to 3.5 range on a 1–5 rating scale. I truly enjoy teaching and try to include as much experiential learning in my courses as is possible. In the future, I would like to teach courses in Organizational Psychology and Team Dynamics.

During the past year, I have served as an intern for the NEO Consulting group. My responsibilities included job analysis, surveys, and feedback of results to management. I believe my consulting experience will help my teaching in bridging the gap between theory and real-world applications.

Thank you for considering my application. If you have any additional questions, please feel free to contact me.

Table 11.3 Master Vita Outline

1. Basic Identifying Information
    a. Name
    b. Date of most recent update
    c. Personal address, phone number, and email
    d. Business address, phone number, and email
    e. Professional certification or licenses
2. Current position, if any
3. Education
    a. Highest degree, school, specialty, and date of completion
        i. Dissertation title and date of completion
    b. Next highest degree, school, specialty, and date of completion
        i. Thesis title and date of completion
    c. Next highest degree, school, specialty, and date of completion
4. Employment
    a. Academic employment, institution, title, and dates
    b. Internships and other applied employment, organization, titles, and dates
    c. Other practical work, such as consulting with a professor
5. Teaching
    a. List courses taught and evaluation scores
6. Publications
    a. Journal articles under review and/or in preparation (particularly important for a graduate student)
    b. Books published or in press
    c. Book chapters published or in press
    d. Journal articles published or in press (peer reviewed)
    e. Other journal articles, reviews, blogs, and non-peer reviewed
7. Conference presentations
8. Grants received and applied for
9. Honors and awards
10. Professional organizations
    a. Committee work
    b. Memberships
11. Editorial boards and reviews for journals or conferences
12. Service
    a. Department
    b. University
    c. Community

For the new graduate, you may want to give additional details on teaching and research experience, but there is no need to overdo it.

You will also need to ask several current faculty to serve as professional references. Select individuals that you have collaborated most closely with throughout graduate school, and that trust not only to praise your ability, but also perhaps more critically, to actually take the time to write the letter and send it off to the schools. Faculty are often overwhelmed with requests for references, so there is no harm in sending friendly reminders of your deadlines.

Those are typically the major components of the application; having covered those, you can submit your package and move on to the next job application. Fair warning, you may never hear from the institution to which you have just applied, as the school might lose funding for the position, or the job might not even exist; stranger things have happened. You may get a rejection as far as a year later when you receive a simple letter stating something along the lines of, "we received many qualified applications, but hired someone else." Saving the best-case scenario for last, your application actually finds its way to the search committee, the search committee is impressed and believes you are a good fit, and invites you in for an interview.

THE INTERVIEW PROCESS

Congratulations! You have received a phone call or an email indicating that you are one of the finalists for a prestigious academic position. As might be expected, academe has its own unique and involved interview process. Although more and more schools have moved to an initial online or phone interview, most still require a lengthy on-campus visit, which can take one to two full days. If you add a day to each end for flying to and from the campus location and include preparation time, a single interview may consume a week of your time. So, three to four interviews will require blocking off a month or more. To make matters worse, this often coincides with the same period when you are trying to finish your dissertation. As a result, this process can be stressful and exhausting, but try to get plenty of rest and relax so that you are able to make a good impression. Your overall presence during these visits will be critical; remember, the people judging you are psychologists.

You may be wondering, how will you fill up a whole day with interviews, or even two days? Your visit will probably involve individual interviews with the search committee, meetings with other program faculty and graduate students, a sit-down with the Dean and other administrators, and a colloquium. Of course, while they are trying to evaluate your worthiness, they are also trying to attract and interest you in the job as well, and provide information you need to determine whether you will accept the job.

The best advice for the interviews, although admittedly vague, is to expect just about anything. However, in all likelihood you will mainly be asked questions concerning your teaching, research, and applied experience, so be prepared to speak on those areas in depth. You should also bring plenty of your own questions concerning expectations of the faculty with teaching, research, and service activities, and the general climate of the department. Areas you definitely want to cover include the types of courses you will be expected to teach, how many courses per semester you will have to teach, what the expectations for tenure are, summer teaching opportunities, and salary.

In terms of the number of courses faculty are expected to teach, this tends to vary between two to four courses per semester for full-time faculty. Basically, for undergraduate only institutions you can expect three to four classes per semester, for master's only institutions you might expect two to three, and at Ph.D. granting institutions, you can expect two per semester. As you can see, the teaching load tends to vary depending on the level of advising responsibilities that you are expected to take on. As a note, you should look beyond the simple number of courses itself, as you could be teaching three small sections of the same course, or two larger sections of different courses which would require more preparation and grading time – these are questions you should ask as well.

As for salary, you can certainly start the conversation, but don't be surprised if you are not given a straightforward answer as to the exact salary offer; the best you can probably hope for is a range. We find it frustrating that institutions often do not wish to reveal salary during the initial interviews, but that appears to be the current state of the world. If you ask the department head about potential salaries, the answer will most likely be "ask the Dean." Then, you can expect the Dean to also avoid the issue.

What are realistic expectations in terms of salary? For current information, a good place to turn is the annual salary surveys conducted by SIOP. At the time we were writing this book, pay for adjunct instructors could be as low as $1,000 to $5,000 per course. The average pay for I-O assistant professors in psychology departments was approximately $70,947, while the average pay for I-Os in business schools was $113,263. When you do receive an offer, keep in mind that academic institutions typically have less room to negotiate than do other employers. That being said, you should know your worth and ask for a higher salary if you feel it is justified, and you can look to the SIOP salary studies to help build your case here.

During your visit, you may be asked to teach a class as well as deliver a colloquium, which refers to "an academic seminar involving a lecture presented by a speaker." In this case, you are the external guest speaker, and the seminar will be attended by faculty and graduate students in the department. Your colloquium presentation will last one to two hours, including questions from the audience. Members of the search committee will be there and psychology faculty from other disciplines such as clinical and experimental will attend. You should expect the unexpected, especially when it comes to unique and challenging questions from your audience.

Normally, your colloquium topic will be based on your dissertation and you may be told that the dissertation must be covered in your colloquium. However, it is wise to demonstrate that you can analyze and interpret data in your colloquium, so if you have not yet collected data from your dissertation, you may want to structure your talk around a few related projects and include the results from additional related research during your presentation. This is also an opportunity to show that you have planned a program of research, of which your dissertation is simply one part. Remember, you will be evaluated not only on the content of your talk, but also on your ability to deliver the content in a way that is accessible to a diverse audience, and engage the audience.

In addition to interviews and the colloquium, you will be scheduled for tours and meals. While much more laid-back than a structured interview, your conduct during meals and happy hours will also be subject to critique. In the past, we have encountered job candidates whose first meal at a fine dining restaurant occurred during their job interviews, which can lead to uncomfortable moments during the dinner. If your manners need polishing, you may want to consider taking an etiquette seminar before embarking on job interviews so that you don't have to worry about manners when you should be focused on the job.

As you prepare to leave at the end of your visit, you should inquire as to when you might receive a decision from the search committee. Of course, in return you may be asked whether you have other interviews and how long you would require arriving at your own decision if offered a job. We would recommend being honest and transparent, with two weeks being a standard period to think about a job offer before providing an official response. In rare cases, you may receive a job offer on the spot and be asked to provide an immediate commitment, in which case the correct response is to politely indicate that you will need time to consider the offer in full.

Hopefully, a desirable offer is made, or several offers, and you decide to accept an offer that you think will be a great fit for you. At that point, you can begin the process of negotiating specifics such as salary, number of classes to be taught, lab space, computers, research funding, and other benefits.

FIRST DAYS, YEARS, AND BEYOND

Starting a new job can be both exhilarating and frightening. You have spent most of your formative years in school, and you will now officially take your place in front of a live classroom. Of course, there is more to the job than teaching, thus, the triumvirate by which you will be judged – teaching, research, and service. Given that you have accepted a full-time, tenure track position, you should be in this job for the long haul, and a good start would be getting to know your colleagues and any students with whom you will be working. Make a point of meeting all the other faculty in the department as well as the staff. The first few years of your job will be the most challenging, and you should plan on working long days to demonstrate your commitment to the department and the profession.

The typical academic career path begins at the level or rank of assistant professor. Universities differ in their timelines, but generally, an assistant professor can expect to serve for four to nine years before being considered for tenure, and to be considered for promotion to associate professor after about five years. At many institutions, the associate and tenure votes are yoked or linked, so that the two decisions are taken at the same time. An individual would then serve another five years after promotion to associate professor and the accompanying granting of tenure, before going up for promotion to full professor. Pay raises during this time are a function of merit and across-the-board increases, with merit judgments being based on teaching, research, and service.

Some faculty choose to diverge from this path to take on leaderships or managerial roles. The typical career ladder in that case would then be department chair, dean, vice president or provost, and at the top, president. A distinction is sometimes made between a chair, who serves at the will of the departmental faculty, and a head, who serves at the will of the dean and provost.

As we mentioned, the first few years in an academic job are the most grueling, especially if on the tenure track. Hopefully, your department is transparent about the requirements for tenure so that you know what to expect from day one and have the time to build a vita that clearly meets the standards. We won't sugarcoat the fact that conducting research is difficult, and publishing in high quality outlets is both time-consuming and risky. This leads to a great deal of pressure on the assistant professor, a phenomenon often referred to as "publish-or-perish," where the perish corresponds to not receiving merit increases, promotions, and tenure. Once you earn tenure, the pressure does lessen significantly. Many individuals prefer not to endure the publish-or-perish gauntlet at all, and choose to apply for and teach at institutions where there is a stronger emphasis on teaching or service, as opposed to research. Additionally, many top-tier programs now require that an assistant professor obtain grants to support their research programs. Attracting grants is challenging in general in psychology, but grant money is especially scarce for I-O Psychology.

*****

If you are pursuing the academic route in I-O Psychology, you have a long road ahead of you. For those who truly love teaching and connecting with aspiring psychologists, you'll find that the challenges of the job, particularly the pre-tenure struggles, are all worth it. While applying for jobs is time-consuming and stressful, you have worked on teaching and research endeavors throughout graduate school that have prepared you for this step in your career. You should come prepared to interviews and carry yourself with professionalism, but also try to be relaxed and honest about your goals so you can find that right fit.

CHAPTER 12

Consulting Jobs and Careers

Welcome passengers, our journey now slowly leaves the world of academe as we enter the exciting land of consulting opportunities. In general, to stay in business, consulting firms sell either their products or the time of their employees. The lifeblood of most firms is billable work and consultants stay green by charging a client for their time.

Approximately 25% of all I-O Psychologists choose to go into the consulting sector. The idea of the consultant lifestyle appeals to many people, especially those that fall more on the extroverted side and have a knack for dealing with diverse groups of individuals. Other appealing features include variety in working on a wide range of projects, making a real difference to your clients, and the opportunity to travel. Hopefully, during your graduate school years, you have made yourself an attractive applicant for consulting jobs by obtaining practical experience, ideally by interning with a consulting firm, although you can certainly draw on other types of applied experience to make yourself a strong candidate.

This chapter covers what you should expect if you decide to pursue a career as a consultant. Specific areas to be covered in this chapter include:

- What are your options?
- When and how to apply.
- The interview process.
- First days, years, and beyond.
- Going at it alone versus with a consulting firm.

In Table 12.1, Jacqueline Carpenter relates the story of how she came to pursue and land a job with a major assessment firm after graduate school.

Table 12.1 Jacqueline Carpenter, Ph.D., A Career in Consulting

When I entered my graduate program, I knew I was interested in becoming an I-O practitioner, but I did not know exactly what that meant. I was fortunate to be enrolled in a program with an engaged alumni network and a strong connection to practitioners in the local area. Though guest lectures from practitioners invited to my classes and our program's weekly invited speaker series, I was able to hear about what it meant to be an I-O Psychologist working at small and large companies, government and non-profit organizations, and consulting firms. I took the opportunity during these events to ask questions about the person's role and the path they took to get there. I researched the companies they worked for and began to form an understanding of the different types of practitioner roles that may be available to me.

I also sought opportunities to be involved in consulting projects through our program's Center for Organizational Research. This afforded me real world experience in a variety of consulting contexts including item writing and development for the public sector, onboarding and training program design for a local non-profit organization, and survey design and analysis for private industry. These experiences helped me understand and prepare for the cycle that characterizes my work as a consultant today; I learned about a client's needs, used my training and expertise to analyze information and create a solution, then, in partnership with a team, delivered or presented that product or service to the client.

I learned about the company I currently work for early in graduate school when one of the company founders, an alumnus of my program, gave a talk during our weekly speaker series. The company's value proposition, to provide a high-fidelity candidate experience as part of a selection assessment, aligned well with my interests in person-organization fit, organizational attraction, and corporate reputation judgments. I had the opportunity to interview for an internship, and was able to draw a connection between the work they do for their clients and the research I was interested in conducting. I interned with Shaker for two years and, due to our mutual interests, I was able to collaborate with them to collect data for my dissertation.

I decided to pursue a full-time position as a consultant in selection because I enjoyed the variety that comes with the job. My job allows me to use my I-O training to develop scientifically rigorous assessments and implement them in a wide variety of organizational settings. Despite working exclusively in assessment for high-volume selection, I am constantly learning about how this function works in different companies, across industries, and across countries. I get to interact daily with I-O practitioners who work at large organizations and with business and HR professionals who have less exposure to our field. The ever-present challenges to meet the unique needs of each client's applicant population, business needs, and work environment appeals to my affinity for puzzles, and I still love learning about the many ways that people work.

WHAT ARE YOUR OPTIONS?

A career in consulting can be especially attractive to a recipient of a master's degree, although there are some firms that give preference to or primarily hire Ph.D.s. As this chapter is being written, a great deal of change is taking place among consulting firms. Many consulting organizations are being acquired by larger firms, some of which have vast holdings outside of human resources, assessment, and I-O Psychology. At the same time, new companies are just starting their existence spurred on by the exciting possibilities offered by new technologies such as virtual and augmented reality.

The very first step in your job search requires looking inward and thinking about what type of consulting job you see yourself in. As mentioned in Chapter 2, there are three main tracks for individuals working in the consulting sector. Individual contributors can be divided into 1) those that work primarily on projects with clients and 2) those that work primarily on research or development, with minimal client contact. Then, there are 3) those who seek out supervisory or managerial roles. Individuals who work primarily with clients can be further divided into individuals who provide services to the client and the unique few who serve as salespeople. Although many consulting firms employ salespeople lacking in technical knowledge, having a degree in I-O Psychology can be a real competitive advantage if you choose to embark on a sales career. That being said, sales does require a certain type of personality, and not everyone is cut out for the uncertainty and requisite risk taking.

Further, you should consider things like the type of firm, and whether you would prefer a small firm with may be up to ten psychologists, or a large firm with hundreds of experts representing a range of specialties. There are so many possible jobs out there that it will help to narrow your search by having a specific type of organization and consulting role in mind when applying.

WHEN AND HOW TO APPLY

Unlike academe, the application and search process for consulting tends to be more compressed. Compared to industry and the public sector, however, consulting firms tend to allow some wiggle room in their timelines when trying to identify and secure talent, and to use more informal search mechanisms. Although you may find consulting positions through job sites such as those offered by SIOP and the Academy of Management, or through employment related websites, our experience has been that consulting firms are more likely to fill their jobs internally, by tapping interns, part-timers, or independent contractors, by raiding other employers, or through informal networks using word of mouth. For that reason, if you are interested in consulting, make sure that your faculty and colleagues know so that they can inform you of any openings they come across.

We would recommend starting to look for jobs with consulting firms about six to nine months in advance of the date you realistically believe you will be able to start a job. You do not want to start too early, as that might land you in an uncomfortable position of being offered a consulting job you cannot accept because of a mismatch in timeline. Use your network to put as many feelers out as possible so that you have a good chance of hearing about it if your dream job opens up. As with any job hunt, those on the market should expect to express interest in many different positions, which can involve a mix of very informal processes and more traditional online application systems. Often, organizations we work with ask us to give them the names of potential candidates, or to have the student contact the organization to initiate the application process.

If there is a firm for which you have always dreamed of working, then go ahead and try to connect with someone there that would be willing to talk with you for an informational interview. However, when dealing with consulting firms it is wise to remember that their lifeblood is billable hours, so service to clients will take priority over your desire for a meet-and-greet. Of course, you should also regularly check the consulting group's employment webpage, as that is probably the best place to find up-to-date information on job openings, as well as instructions for applying.

Once you hear about an opening and start that process, you will be asked to fill out an application. If the organization follows a more formal process, the company will also request a cover letter and a résumé. Note that we said résumé intentionally; while vitas are used in the academic world, most jobs outside of educational settings ask you to provide a much more condensed document in the form of a résumé. Business people with 30 years of corporate experience have one-page résumés, so if you are just getting out of school, you do not need a ten-page résumé. For a recent graduate, we would recommend a one- to two-page résumé at most, with emphasis on trying for one page if possible. You can save the more detailed explanations for the cover letter or for the interview. A sample résumé appears in Table 12.2.

Another part of the application package is a cover letter. We would recommend attaching one if you can, even if it is not explicitly required. This is an opportunity to discuss your background and potential fit for the position in more detail than a few bulleted points on a résumé. Our advice

Table 12.2 Sample Résumé

Margaret Follies
Psychology Department
University of Stow
Stow, OH 44,224
mfollies@ustow.edu
10/5/2018

Consulting and Applied Experience

Intern for NEO Consulting Group, *September 2017 – Present.*

- Responsibilities included job analysis, surveys, and feedback of results to management.

Intern for Hennessey Restaurants and Hotels, *May 2017 – September 2017.*

- Designed and evaluated a customer service training program.

Consultant for Center for Applied Experience, University of Stow,
May 2016 – Present.

- Completed several projects for large and small companies, and the public sector, including work in job analysis, test development, and statistical analysis.

Education

Ph.D., Industrial-Organizational Psychology
May 2019 (Expected), University of Stow.

M.S., General Psychology
May 2015, University of Stow.

B.S., Psychology
May 2013, Walsh University.

Academic and Teaching Experience

Teaching Assistant, Introduction to Psychology, University of Stow, *September 2013 – May 2017.*

Lecturer, Social Science Statistics, Wayne Community College, *Summer 2016.*

Select Publications and Presentations

Follies, M., & Speaker, L.D. (2018). Organizational persuasion and individual outcomes. *The Journal of Personnel Assessment and Decisions.*

Speaker, L.D. & Follies, M. (2017). Challenges and new directions in organizational persuasion research. *Poster presented at Society for Industrial and Organizational Psychology Conference.*

Additional Training
- Fluent in Russian and Chinese.
- Knowledge of SPSS and R programming language.

Other Interests
- Field hockey; was captain Walsh University team.
- Golf.

would be to prepare a generic cover letter for your job search, but then to modify the cover letter to fit the requirements of each specific position of interest. For the newly minted Ph.D., this letter will be one to two pages long and include the following paragraphs:

1. Formal indication of interest and application for the position. A brief statement of why you are qualified for the position.
2. Review of internships, applied work, and practical experiences.
3. Review of educational background, including expected date of completion of degree if it is still in progress.
4. Short review of research experience and interests and very brief mention of teaching.
5. Thank you.

In other words, the letter could be very similar to the academic cover letter in Table 11.3., but with a greater emphasis on your consulting experience, and should provide a lot more detail on some of your major projects and work assignments.

You may also be asked for references, but rather than requiring that written documents be sent in or uploaded by your references, the organization would more likely indicate that they will call or email your references if further information is needed. Even if you put references down to receive a call rather than asking them to write a letter, make a point to notify and ask permission of your references.

Assessment firms in particular may ask you to take a battery of their own tests or assessments. At first, you may find this strange. You may think to yourself "I know what the tests are looking for, why would they ask me to take this battery of tests?" However, if you think about it, requiring you to take the tests does make good sense. The perspective of the firm is that if they really believe a battery of assessments is useful in identifying the best and brightest among candidates, and those with the best fit, then actions speak louder than words and they should administer their own suite of assessments for when making their own hiring decisions.

THE INTERVIEW PROCESS

Congratulations, after submitting your application, you have received a phone call or an email indicating that the organization, or hopefully multiple organizations, would like to bring you in for an interview. This is a stressful but exciting place to be. Consulting firms may use a multiple hurdle approach in their interviews, bringing you back several times, with the length of the interviews and the organizational level of the inter-viewers increasing each time. Naturally you should review the job description, be prepared to answer behavioral questions about past experi-ences that tie into the job, and discuss your strengths, areas of expertise, and goals. You should also be prepared to be drilled in at least one of the interviews with regard to your technical knowledge of I-O Psychology, which may give you flashbacks to comprehensive examinations. For example, if interviewing with an assessment firm, you might be asked a series of questions about how to test for adverse impact or the different theories of discrimination. At this time, you will thank your professors for making life hard for you back in the early graduate school days.

Assessment centers, work samples, or role plays may be a part of one of your visit days. You might be given a set of computer printouts and asked to write a short report and then present it to a simulated client. Or, you might be given assessment data indicating that a manager has significant deficiencies and be required to conduct a feedback session. The best advice for your visits is to expect just about anything. Of course, interviewers want you to succeed and you should feel free to ask questions about what you are in for and how to best prepare.

Remember that the hiring process is a two-way street. Both parties are trying to assess whether the job would be a good match. You should take an inquisitive approach and gather as much information as you can about the company, role, expectations, and culture when it is your turn to ask questions. Particularly in the consulting arena, we would recommend paying close attention to fit, which is probably more important to success and happiness in consulting than in any other sectors. Consider fit with the organizational culture, your fit with your likely supervisor, and your fit with the other new consultants. We can guarantee that the organization is also carefully considering to what extent you fit with their culture, with what their clients look for in a consultant, and with the role they would like you to fill.

Some areas you should make a point to gain clarity on include what type of role will you be asked to fill, how often will you be expected to travel, whether trips home will be covered when traveling for extended periods, and how many hours you will be expected to work per week. Frequent travel is more likely to be required when working for large firms, although we have known many small consultants that service a global clientele. If you are catching onto a theme, good job. The life of a consultant often involves extended days, long weeks, and frequent travel, although this is certainly not the case in all consulting jobs.

What are realistic expectations in terms of salary? For current information, a good place to turn would be the salary surveys conducted by SIOP. At the time we were writing this book, the average entry-level salaries in consulting were $115,000 for doctorates and $73,000 for master's. Median income for those with doctorates in consulting organizations was $135,000, $83,000 for those with master's degrees. Consulting is the most difficult area in which to give advice as to what to expect or negotiate for in terms of pay, because a large portion of your salary may be dependent upon your ability to bill clients and the overall profitability of the consulting organization. As a result, you may be quoted what appears at first glance to be a lower salary, although the typical employee in the organization receives substantial bonuses during the year.

As you prepare to leave at the end of your visit, you should inquire as to what will come next, whether there are additional visits to be scheduled or you should expect to receive some type of offer. You should send a thank you note to your interviewers and a friendly follow up if you have not heard back after the allotted time. Hopefully, a desirable offer is made and you decide to accept. At that point, you can begin the process of negotiating specifics such as salary and start date. Remember that there is likely more wiggle room to negotiate salary in consulting than in other sectors.

FIRST DAYS, YEARS, AND BEYOND

Consulting firms we have worked with often try to bring their new employees along slowly the first few months, letting them get their feet wet and adjust to the job. Although, having said that, we would bet there are employers that use a "feet to the fire" strategy. This totally depends on the firm and overall culture, which hopefully you were able to gather a realistic impression of so that you know what to expect walking into this new job.

As one of the newbies, you may find yourself writing and responding to requests for proposals, or RFPs, and performing basic tasks such as job analysis. Do not get discouraged if assigned what seem to be clerical or less exciting tasks, because taking them on shows that you can be a team player. This is especially true in smaller firms where you will see everyone pitching in from time to time to make sure deadlines are met and work completed. At the same time, from the perspective of the relatively new employee, we would advise seeking out developmental experiences that expand your knowledge base and increase your visibility both internally and with clients.

Evaluation of performance in consulting tends to be pretty straightforward for those with the more standard client-facing roles. Your clients either like your work or they do not, and this should be clear to you. You generate billable hours or you do not. You convince clients to purchase additional services and hours or you do not. You make money for the firm or you do not. From that perspective, what constitutes success is much more objective than in the other sectors. So, if you see that this type of job is not a good match for you, you should be able to realize it fairly quickly and consider whether you would be better suited to a different role or another sector.

As individuals advance in their careers, they may choose to take on supervisory and managerial responsibilities, or they may prefer to become even more specialized through the development of expertise in select areas. The ability to move between different functional roles will be dictated by the culture and size of the organization, as smaller firms will be flatter with fewer managers. This is also something you should consider in the interview stage if it is important to you to have some flexibility in your role or even to be able to change roles.

GOING AT IT ALONE VERSUS JOINING A CONSULTING FIRM

Consulting offers a choice not available in the academic, industry, or public sector. That is, instead of applying for a job and working for someone else, you can hang out your shingle as an independent consultant offering a service directly to clients. You can do this alone or with a few colleagues from graduate school. Eventually, if you attract enough work, you can hire other individuals to assist you and start to build a consulting firm.

For some people that naturally have the entrepreneurial spirit, working for yourself may seem very attractive. Consulting on your own offers an almost unlimited monetary ceiling, as you can charge whatever the market will bear, and you get to keep whatever clients pay you for your services, or at least what is left after you pay your taxes and social security. You are your own boss, so you can make your own hours and work as much or as little as you want, from anywhere you want.

Not to burst your bubble too quickly, but we should be fair and discuss potential downsides as well. As an independent consultant, you need to be strong in communicating your value, as you will be doing a lot of selling of your services to organizations and drafting replies to requests for proposals, which will also consume time that could otherwise have resulted in billable hours. You will have monthly expenses including rent and other office costs, health and professional insurance payments, utilities, and a host of other recurring monthly fees and charges. Clients may take months to pay you, or even years, or never pay you at all.

This is a tough road for someone right out of a master's or Ph.D. program, but if you think this route is for you, we wish you the best. Our recommendation would be that a relatively new professional should first gain a certain amount of practical work experience, a reputation as a reliable service provider, and also generate a network of contacts. This can be accomplished by working for an established consulting firm for a year or two, or by taking a job in industry or the public sector. It would also be beneficial to meet with a consultant that can help you work on your "sales pitch," marketing, and attracting new leads, which are skills that most people were not exposed to in graduate school.

In recent years, adding a practice in executive or leadership coaching to one's practitioner toolbox has become a popular option for the sole practitioner. Business coaches can work one-on-one or in small groups with managers, leaders, and executives in order to help them expand their competencies and achieve and obtain success. Primarily, the coaching process involves counseling-type sessions where the coach works with the client on communication, goal-setting, action planning, and overcoming weaknesses. Unfortunately, most graduate programs do not offer coaching courses, so if this sounds appealing to you, you should consider enrolling in supplemental or online courses, such as individual assessment, or even the possibility of attaining a coaching certification (see Chapter 9 and Table 9.1). Another option would be to join the Society of Consulting Psychology, Division 13 of the American Psychological Association, which puts on an annual conference that offers a large number of workshops and sessions on coaching psychology.

*****

As you can see, there are a lot of career paths you can take even within consulting, which is something you should think about extensively before beginning a job search. Think about what you are good at and what type of work excites and motivates you, as bringing this to your job interviews will help you find a role that you enjoy. When you start to get interviews, do your research and come prepared, but also consider it an information-gathering session for yourself. If you do decide to go at it alone, it will be challenging, but at least you will avoid the hassle of interviewing for jobs!

CHAPTER 13

Industry Jobs and Careers

As noted in Chapter 2, the term "industry" can be regarded as archaic, a leftover from the golden age of large American manufacturers; however, it still conforms to the standard labeling of the four sectors. The term "industry" is used to refer to private sector companies, which includes businesses as diverse as those in banking, finance, health care, information technology, retail, and manufacturing.

Approximately 25% of all I-O Psychologists are in the industrial sector, which is the same percentage as for consulting. Some are drawn to this path because life in industry is typically more orderly, involving a standard work schedule and less travel, although this many not always be the case, especially when working for large, global entities. There are a lot of types of jobs and companies within the industry sector, but across the board a common challenge in this setting is trying to maintain one's professional identity.

This chapter covers the basics of applying for an industry job and what to expect if you do decide to pursue a career in industry. Areas to be covered in this chapter include:

- What are your options?
- When and how to apply.
- The interview process.
- First days, years, and beyond.

Accompanying this chapter are two personal stories. In Table 13.1, Gina Seaton shares an intriguing and humorous tale of her job hunt in the industrial sector, in which analogies are drawn to the process of dating. In Table 13.2, Drew Lam, who has worked in two jobs with manufacturers located in the Midwest and has acquired quite a bit of career wisdom, relates his views on what it is like to work in industry.

Table 13.1 Gina Seaton, Ph.D., Dating Jobs and Landing an Industry Job

For most of my education, I was unsure of what I wanted to be when I grew up. Needless to say, my path to becoming an I-O took a little longer than usual. I started by seeking a master's degree in I-O Psychology. Once I was finished, I realized that I still was not quite ready to grow up yet and continued on to a Ph.D. program. While this did add time onto my journey, I like to think there was a silver lining to not having a firm grasp on knowing where my career was heading. I spent a *lot* of time exploring my options. I straddled the academic vs. practitioner train as long as possible and devoted roughly equal time to research, teaching, and gaining applied experience in both external consulting and corporate HR settings. Essentially, I said "yes" to almost every opportunity available to me, seeking vertical development opportunities whenever possible. These varied experiences were paramount in helping me carve out my career path. I learned a lot about myself including what I was/was not good at and what I enjoyed/did not enjoy. Most importantly, I learned that I would not be happy in a job unless I felt like I could say I was truly adding value with my specific I-O expertise. This realization set the tone for my job search activities, and for me, this meant focusing my search on more traditional I-O roles within selection, assessment, and applied research.

When people tell you searching for jobs is like dating, believe them, because that is exactly what it is like. It takes a significant amount of time, you court a lot of organizations, and you are both covertly trying to figure out how many other people the other is seeing. You also expend a lot of energy "primping" for the date (interview), except this primping takes years instead of minutes (or hours). For me, a large portion of the primping efforts that landed me the second date (interview) were those same varied experiences that helped me figure out what I wanted to do with my life. Varied experiences played a significant role in fashioning me into a well-rounded practitioner of I-O Psychology. Prospective employers liked that I had worn some different hats and would be able to pull from those experiences to navigate complexities in their organizations. For example, while the roles I applied to focused on selection, assessment, and applied research, many of the teams had undergone some kind of restructuring in recent months and felt my experience in change management would be an asset.

A second area that was vital to landing a second interview (date) was coursework. In my experience, interviews started like a typical first date with some casual, light-hearted conversation where you try to make a good impression on one another. But, instead of ending the date with some mutually enjoyable activity (like dinner or a movie), you take a selection, research methods, and tests and measures final exam. A majority of the questions (and in some instances, all of the questions) I was asked in the interviews were technical in nature. *How do you perform a validation study? Walk me through the process of developing an assessment. What are all of the different ways you can look for adverse impact?* These questions drew on many years of learning from multiple courses. Fortunately, I had excellent instructors and paid attention in class (Thanks, Dennis!).

Soon, I start my new role as an I-O Psychologist. Getting here took a lot of time and effort. There were many times I thought graduate school would never end (but also a lot of times I *wished* it would never end). All the time and hard work was worth it, though, because I truly think I have found "the one" as far as first jobs go. I wouldn't have been qualified for the particular job I got right out of graduate school if I had not had taken advantage of opportunities to gain varied experience and made the most out of occasions to build in-depth technical knowledge. Even if you are more fortunate than I and know early on what kind of I-O you want to be when you grow up, my advice remains the same: be hungry for opportunities and expose yourself to as much as you can in graduate school.

Table 13.2 Drew Lam, Ph.D., A Career in Industry

I have always held a growth mindset, so getting to this spot in my career by no means indicates that I am a success. Rather, it indicates a single point-in-time snapshot of where I am in my development. My story of what got me to this point is different than most traditional routes. I did a lot of things you shouldn't do to be successful.

Here is a brief checklist:

- Average GRE scores
- Went to the graduate program at my undergraduate university
- No publications
- Took teaching assistantships over internships
- Incorporated and ran a youth soccer club in my free time

Despite doing things the "wrong way," I was able to land a first job opportunity that set me up well for my career. How exactly did this happen?

I had the fortune to have Dr. Dennis Doverspike as a graduate advisor who was an advocate for me. Dating back to my undergraduate days, Dennis was the faculty member who believed I could be successful. In graduate school, Dennis would include me on consulting projects where I would get applied experience. I used every project as an opportunity to demonstrate my knowledge and expertise. The consulting projects included job analysis, test proctoring, engagement surveys, and data analysis. With each opportunity, I made it a point to demonstrate professionalism, leadership, and ability to produce a high-quality deliverable.

Outside of the consulting work, I demonstrated leadership in other areas. As a teaching assistant, beyond delivering high-energy, engaging classes, I took the opportunity to mentor many current and former students in their career goals and graduate school pursuits. In my fourth year as an instructor I was recognized and awarded our University's Outstanding Graduate Teaching Assistant award, which recognized knowledge, teaching and motivational skills, creativity, and learner-centeredness. Although teaching was not related to anything specific that I would do in my future job, being recognized as one of the best and leading others were areas where I made teaching something more than my peers.

Another interest outside of my studies was soccer. I picked up coaching which eventually turned into building a youth non-profit, 501(c)(3) status, premier soccer club. I found myself volunteering my time running a soccer club. Every other weekend it felt like I was traveling to some obscure Midwest city to coach or running a board meeting. In the end, I took the opportunity to get involved in something that I was passionate about at the time and was able to give back to my community and demonstrate leadership.

I built a lot of genuine connections in graduate school, which proved to be helpful in finding a job. One of those connections was with a classmate who was working a few years in the field prior to me hitting the job market. At the time she was looking for an analyst to work for her and invited me to interview for the role. The role was much broader than my past consulting experiences. In order to compensate for my lack of experience, to prepare for my interview, I applied my past experiences in my classes, consulting, teaching, and coaching to the position that I was interviewing for. While my consulting and coursework could help me to answer the technical questions, I found that it was my teaching and coaching experiences that helped me the most. Anybody moving on to the interview stage has the appropriate technical background; however, conceptualizing my experiences as demonstration of competencies for success in applied settings (e.g. leadership, professionalism, ambition, drive, and growth mindset) were the most important for me landing that first job.

I have since moved on to different roles at other companies, but I am grateful for my first big break. I now am proud to serve as the Senior Manager Organization Development at Shearer's Snacks, which is a leading contract manufacturer and private label supplier for the snack industries.

To summarize, do not do what I did. But if you do find yourself in a similar situation, in that you lack the exact experience required for the position that you are pursuing, my advice is to translate your actual experiences to the competencies needed to be successful in the role. Once you have the role, you will learn from your boss and peers, and you will return the favor by teaching them what you know from all your years of school and previous work experiences.

WHAT ARE YOUR OPTIONS?

A career in industry can be especially attractive to a recipient of a master's degree; in fact, a Ph.D., might be considered over-qualified for many jobs in this sector, although larger companies with dedicated I-O teams do tend to hire Ph.D. graduates. Individuals with I-O backgrounds in industry usually take on either the role of a specialist in an area such as selection or performance management, or function as a human resource generalist. Specialists may serve as internal consultants, which can require selling their services to other areas of the organization in order to stay viable. As with the other sectors, the individual I-O Psychologist may seek promotions into management positions or prefer to remain an advanced specialist or expert individual contributor throughout their career.

Think about what area you could contribute to or specialize in, and whether you would rather be the person with in-depth knowledge in one area or have insight into a wider variety of I-O practices in an organization. Industry, company size, whether they already employ a team of I-O professionals, and culture are also attributes that can help you find your best fit in a job search.

WHEN AND HOW TO APPLY

At least for entry-level jobs, the timeline for application for the industrial sector is more compact, narrow, and set than for consulting or academe (As a note, although we use the term "entry-level," it is probably a misnomer in that some use entry-level to refer to clerical jobs, whereas we are using the term to refer to associate, specialist, and even managerial positions). Because of this shorter hiring process, you should refrain from applying for an industrial job until closer to the time that you plan to enter the workforce. You might start asking for informational interviews a year ahead of time, but you should be reasonably close to finishing up your degree, or at least to being able to start work, before you start applying. We would recommend two to six months in advance of your ideal start date. An argument could even be made for waiting until you have completed your scholastic responsibilities to begin the job search, but this will completely depend on your preferences and needs at the time that you are wrapping up your degree.

Where you should look for jobs will be a function of your degree level. If you have a doctorate, you will probably have more luck and find more appropriate listings on job sites such as those offered by SIOP and the Academy of Management, especially the SIOP JobNet. Consideration should also be given to attending the annual SIOP conference, which features a job placement center. Another excellent source of information on job openings is the Society for Human Resource Management (SHRM). SHRM has a website where you can search for human resource jobs through a large database, and filter options by your expertise, location, or other specifications. If pursuing work in the private sector, it would be smart investment to join SHRM. Of course, you should also utilize informal networks, so make sure that faculty and colleagues know of your interest in industry jobs.

If there is a firm you have always dreamed of working for, connect with someone there and go ahead and try to set up an informational interview. You should also regularly check the organization's employment webpage, as that is probably the best place to find up-to-date information on job openings, as well as instructions for applying.

At the master's level, there is no harm in searching the SIOP job site; however, it is unlikely to yield many of the HR generalist type of positions you may be seeking. Luckily, there are a large number of employment related search engines to which you can subscribe. Once you express an interest by subscribing to one, you will no doubt receive emails from five more search engines, and before you know it, your inbox will be full of daily emails recommending a host of human resource jobs to you.

In the process of writing this book, we subscribed to a number of the employee search engines. On any given morning, we can open our inboxes and find notices regarding 20 to 30 human resource jobs, a number of which could be appropriate for a person with a master's degree in I-O Psychology seeking their first job. Many of the positions are in the northeast Ohio area, where we are located, but others are in cities across the country, and we also see human resource jobs that are remote or involving telecommuting.

At the Ph.D. level, contacting a headhunter would be another possibility, especially if you have been able to gain industrial experience through internships or post-docs. Headhunters are a type of executive and upper-level managerial recruiter, who identify and recommend prospective candidates to companies. The headhunter's fee is usually paid by the organization. Although headhunters technically work for the employer, our experience has been that they are eager to identify qualified candidates who they can then recommend to multiple companies. If you are interested in going this route, then ask your faculty or some associates in industry jobs if they could recommend or connect you with any headhunters.

Even a small employer of I-O Psychologists in the industrial sector will be larger than all but the biggest consulting firms. As a result, you can expect the job application process to be more formal than that used by consulting organizations. The process will include completing a lengthy online application, and uploading a résumé and cover letter. Thanks to the success enjoyed by our field, you may also be required to complete an assessment battery including a variety of pre-employment tests. Regarding your résumé, we reiterate our advice from applying to jobs in consulting: if you are just getting out of school, you do not need a ten-page résumé; you can save your detailed explanations for the cover letter or for the interview. At most, for a recent graduate, we would recommend a one- to two-page résumé, with emphasis on trying for one page. A sample résumé appears in Table 12.2.

THE INTERVIEW PROCESS

A letter or email arrives informing you that you have been selected for an interview with a large industrial concern. You should expect the interview process to take a multiple hurdle approach, where if successful during your first visit, you are then brought back for additional days of interviews. The intensity of the interviews will probably increase over time, although so may the attempts of the company to seduce you into accepting an offer. If you are looking for a generalist job at the master's level, hopefully you have made yourself an attractive applicant through applied experience or an internship.

Over the years, we have often heard past graduates with master's degrees gripe about having interviewed but never hearing back from the company or were not receiving offers after interviewing. It may just be an issue of patience as it takes time to find the right fit and may involve applying for more jobs than you imagined, or broadening your specifications. In reply to those experiencing some of these issues, here is our advice:

- You are going to have to apply for a large number of jobs in order to receive a small number of interviews.
- You may have to sell the company on an I-O background. The individuals doing the hiring may not know what I-O Psychology is or why it would prepare you for a human resource job as a generalist or in a specialty area. In your cover letter and in the interview, you will to have to sell and tell regarding I-O and demonstrate why your educational background is the ideal one for the job.
- Perform an honest self-assessment and evaluation to determine whether your search is realistic. Do you have the skills that companies would look for in the role? Have you done an internship? Can

you speak business lingo? Do you have familiarity with other business areas like budgeting and finance? Do you read *The Wall Street Journal*? If you identify a gap, you can adjust your search by developing your own skills or applying for different types of jobs.

- Have you done your homework on the company? Do you know the company's mission statement and what their major products are? Do you have a sense of the organization's strengths, weaknesses, opportunities, and threats?

- Have you done your homework on the company's major products? If the organization makes light bulbs, learn how lamps are manufactured. If the firm rebuilds diesel engines, find out how engines are rebuilt.

- Are you an effective interviewee? When seeking a job in industry, especially for master's level candidates, you need to make a good first and last impression in the interview by presenting an image that shows you will be a great fit and a solid contributor in the organization. If you are granted interviews, but never seem to be offered a job, consider recording yourself doing a simulated interview, and then ask a faculty member, friend, or respected colleague to critique your performance.

- Be careful of appearing too assertive, aggressive, or defensive. It's great to show ambition, but there is no reason to tell your future boss that you will soon have their job. If you make errors, or do not know the answer to a question, be willing to admit that you do make mistakes.

TEXTBOX 13.1 PROJECT A WELL-ROUNDED IMAGE

In a survey we conducted for SIOP, a unique feature of industry interviews was the tendency to look for individuals who had participated in extracurricular activities, conducted research, been active in publishing and conferences, and could best be described as well-rounded.

At some point in the sequence of interviews, you will want to ask questions covering areas like salary, vacation days, and benefits. What are realistic expectations in terms of salary? For current information, a good place to turn is the annual salary surveys conducted by SIOP. At the time we were writing this book, the median income for doctorates in industry-manufacturing was $140,000. With master's, the median was $86,000. At entry, salaries were $75,000 for doctorates and $74,000 for master's. At the managerial level, the salaries were $152,000 for doctorates and $120,000 for master's. Giving exact advice on negotiating a starting salary is complicated, in that some type of bonus pay is common in the industrial sector.

As you prepare to leave at the end of your visit, you should inquire as to what will come next, whether there are additional visits to be scheduled or you should expect to receive some type of offer. Hopefully, a desirable offer is made, and you decide to accept. At that point, you can begin the process of negotiating specifics such as salary and start date.

FIRST DAYS, YEARS, AND BEYOND

As indicated in the beginning of the chapter, you are likely to find yourself working as a human resource generalist, in a specialized department such as training or organization development, or serving as an internal consultant. Depending on the size and history of the organization, you may be the only person with an I-O background, or one member of a large team of I-O professionals. At one time, it was common for larger organizations to employ a cadre of I-O Psychologists who worked together as a team on cutting-edge practical research projects, but in these days of cost cutting and lean organizations, those large internal research teams are a rare commodity, a throwback to a bygone age. Your supervisor may be an expert in I-O or be totally in the dark as to what someone with an I-O background can bring to the table.

What will your first few days or months on the job be like? There are so many ways this could go depending on the job and the organization, but we hope that you have gathered a good picture of this throughout the interview process and can walk into your first day knowing exactly what to expect. However, this is not always the case. We could tell you a lot of strange stories, but due to space constraints we will just mention a few. We have heard of companies that believed that new employees, especially those in management or human resources, should first get a feel of what it is like to do the jobs that pay the bills; sort of an onboarding version of *Undercover Boss*. A home improvement company we worked with would require all new employees, including I-O Psychologists, to go door-to-door in the toughest sales regions trying to sell their products and services. Now, clearly that would not work if you are hired by a hospital, but there are still those companies that believe in the old-fashioned "start in the mail room" model of onboarding new employees.

The other extreme is new hires who are given a project that everyone else refuses to take on or is always pushed off on the new employees. Or, even more challenging, an assignment that far exceeds your education and experience. If on your first day you are told "your goal for the next six months is to develop a global, pre-employment selection system that is low cost, has extremely high validity, and results in no adverse impact," well, at that point you better have a talk with your supervisor to set more realistic expectations, start sending your résumé out to other organizations, or ask for an immediate pay raise. Of course, you could always ask for a large budget and then hire one of your friends who went into consulting.

If you are lucky, you will land in a job where the organization understands the importance of carefully bringing their new hires along by offering a range of progressive, developmental experiences. Hopefully, you have a manager who serves as an effective professional and business mentor.

As mentioned in the beginning of this chapter, one of the challenges you may face is maintaining your personal identity as an I-O Psychologist. Your organization may not appreciate the value in attending professional conferences or subscribing to journals. From a career perspective, you may find that the fastest way to advance is to rotate through other types of managerial specialties, acquiring a broad business background, and competencies in line operations, sales, accounting, and other managerial functions. Doing so will have the effect of reducing the degree of attachment to the field of I-O. This is a personal decision you will have to face, does your future lie in identifying as an I-O professional, or in developing as a manager? Do not despair, many others before you have faced the same dilemma.

You may even find that advancing up the management ladder requires you to pursue work with other employers. Another possible path is to move between consulting firms and industrial organizations. The benefit of switching back and forth is that spending time with a consulting firm allows one to acquire experience in diverse areas in a shorter period of time. Thus, you will encounter individuals who started with a consulting firm, were then recruited by a client company, and then completed the circle by returning to consulting.

*****

There are so many ways to harness your I-O training for a successful and lucrative career in industry. Those that go this route may just be trying it out to see what they like, or they may be attracted to the aspects of stability, working with the same people and seeing the impact of your work, and having a wider range of activities and opportunities available when you are the I-O expert in an organization. Some people have trouble with the job search, but we find that good candidates do land great jobs with time and persistence. If you are considering this type of career, we hope this chapter has given you a balanced perspective of what you can expect.

CHAPTER 14

Government Jobs and Careers

Public sector motivation theory suggests there are individuals who possess a need to serve the public, and to work in occupations where they can do good and advance society toward more noble goals. For many millennials, the events of 9/11 were a generational turning point, leading to a desire to enter government service as an avenue for expressing their patriotism or working to create a better world. For others, government jobs offer a unique combination of job security, especially compared to the industrial sector, and generous benefits.

Regardless of the underlying motivation, there are people who are attracted to working for the government, and you may be one of those individuals who have decided that you would like to pursue a career in the public sector. Approximately 10% of all I-O Psychologists are in the government sector, which is the smallest proportion for a sector. This chapter covers the basics of applying for a government job and what to expect if you do decide to pursue a career in industry. Areas to be covered in this chapter include:

- What are your options?
- When and how to apply.
- The interview process.
- First days, years, and beyond.

Accompanying this chapter, in Table 14.1, is a career perspective by George Vaughn, who found his calling in public sector work and shares his perspective on the challenges and benefits of working in government.

Table 14.1 George Vaughn, M.A., A Career in the Public Sector

First, I think it's important to put my public sector experience into context. I came to a moderately large county that had recently undergone a dramatic change in its form of government. Employment practices received a major overhaul, including the creation of a new, independent civil service commission. My role was straightforward: build a testing operation that both ensured the county's compliance with employment laws while also rising above the stereotype of the stale, generic civil service process that is often a tradition in local government. I came from a background of consulting primarily for the public sector, so I was familiar with government requirements and felt prepared for the environment.

Well, prepare for the bureaucracy typical of government roles. While any I-O strives to meet federal guidelines and professional best practices, state and local governments have additional and often very specific civil services laws. Processes are less flexible, and change takes more approvals (and more time). This is frustrating for all the stakeholders, and practitioners can be the targets of those frustrations. Most I-Os doing the frontline job analysis and test development need a lot of patience, both for processes outside their control and for the reactions of the hiring managers.

When a government agency comes to you as a consultant, it's usually for one of two reasons: they want your help, or they need your help. Either way, you must be prepared to market yourself and what you can bring to the client. This doesn't stop once you're in the organization, and in a number of ways, it can be worse. Many of your clients don't think they need your help, and they certainly don't want it. They aren't familiar with I-O Psychology, and they feel forced into a process that takes away their autonomy. The first temptation is to point at civil service requirements, tell them it's the law, and go about your business. However, it takes creativity and an honest look at how they feel and what they need to move forward.

Once you overcome those obstacles, you begin to see the real benefits of working in government: your successes directly impact your own organization. While you may move on to the next task at hand, your previous work improves the organization around you. You essentially have a captive client base, but when managers reap the rewards of your expertise, the relationships become more positive and trusting. The next project becomes a little easier. The capability of the department becomes a little better. And as a citizen, you know firsthand that your government is a little better at providing needed services to the area. You reap benefits as an employee and a taxpayer.

WHAT ARE YOUR OPTIONS?

As mentioned in Chapter 2, the government sector includes a wide range of potential employers from the federal government, state and local jurisdictions, various federal and state agencies, to even the military. There are also quasi-sector public sector agencies such as the Post Office, state universities, and local transit authorities and utilities that employ I-O Psychologists.

For I-O jobs, the minimum qualification is usually a master's degree, although a unique feature of government agencies, especially the federal government, is that formal degree attainment is often de-emphasized. As with industry, there tends to be a correlation between the size of the government jurisdiction and the probability of employing individuals with doctorates. The U.S. government and its many associated agencies are more likely to seek and employ Ph.D.s. At the state level and for larger cities and counties, a master's degree often serves as the minimum qualification. In smaller cities, many assessment positions may be held by individuals with bachelor's degrees, or even individuals whose highest level of education is high school who have landed their position by working their way up. A career in government can be especially attractive to a recipient of a master's degree; outside of the federal government, a Ph.D. might be considered over-qualified for many jobs in this sector.

In terms of career roles and ladders, there is a great deal of similarity to industry roles. Individuals with I-O backgrounds take on either the role of a specialist, for example in assessment or organization development, or function as a human resource generalist. As with the other areas, the individual I-O Psychologist may seek promotions into management positions or prefer to remain an advanced specialist or expert individual contributor throughout their career. A major difference between the industry and the government sectors, is that managers in the public sector or more like to retain their professional identification and continue to serve as an expert in their specialty area. So, as you see, you can have a lot of different roles in government and if going this route, you still have some decisions to make as to what type of agency and role you are best suited for.

WHEN AND HOW TO APPLY

The public sector has the most regimented, strictest timelines for jobs. In part, this is driven by various government regulations as well as requirements that hiring be transparent and open. In the public sector, jobs are usually posted on a specific date, with a very strict deadline for receipt of applications and established rules for determining the most meritorious candidate. Being offered a position usually requires taking and being one of the high scorers on a competitive examination. The testing process may involve an objective, multiple-choice job knowledge test or an evaluation of training and experience based on the completion of a questionnaire. The process also is likely to involve highly structured interviews with individuals or panels.

As with other sectors, where you should look for jobs will be a function of your degree level. If you have a doctorate, you should consider the SIOP and Academy of Management job sites. At the master's level, you should consider subscribing to any of the large number of available employment related search engines.

There are a number of organizations and sites offering public sector postings. The SHRM job search platform includes government positions in their job listings. The International Public Management Association for Human Resources (IPMA-HR) represents public sector human resource professionals at federal, state, and local level government organizations. Thus, IPMA-HR might be considered a public sector parallel of SHRM. IPMA also offers a job posting service and a jobs webpage, which is an excellent source of information for a search within the government sector.

Another professional organization is the International Personnel Assessment Council (IPAC). One of the member benefits is a job board, which features a variety of assessment postings, including ones for internships. Another worthy of mention is the Personnel Testing Council Metropolitan Washington (PTCMW). Given its Washington base of operations, an attractive feature of the PTCMW's job listings is the large number of positions with the Federal government and its agencies. For Federal jobs in particular, you should also perform a search at USAJOBS.

Although you may still find some smaller government agencies that require you to present yourself in person and complete a paper application, most jobs will use an online application procedure. However, due to security concerns, relatively few jurisdictions use an online testing portal. Therefore, you may be required to sit for a group examination.

THE INTERVIEW PROCESS

As previously discussed, the interview process in the public sector tends to be more structured and objective. Your interview performance will be scored and added to any other required assessments in order to arrive at a ranking of candidates based on merit, from which final hiring decisions are made. Thus, you need to ace your interview.

Along with structured questions, another unique feature of the public-sector interview is that it is often conducted by a panel of subject matter experts; thus the name "panel interview." If the panel members are not there live and in person, the interview may be recorded for later rating by experts. You should expect to have to discuss your job knowledge and past experience, along with questions where you are asked to demonstrate your competency in decision-making, teamwork, and leadership.

Some government jobs, depending on the level of sensitivity of the work, may have citizenship requirements and involve extensive background checks to attain a certain required level of security clearance. Further, you could be asked to take drug tests and physical health assessments. You should be aware of this, as logistically it can be a lengthy process, and some people are turned off by employers who cross into the boundary of the personal life, but it comes with the territory of government work.

Discussion of salary and benefits may not occur until after you have received an offer. What are realistic expectations in terms of salary? Salaries in government trend lower than salaries in the other sectors. The average salary for doctorates employed with the federal government was $119,00, while for those with master's $100,000. The average salary for doctorates employed with state governments was $102,000, while for those with master's $68,000. Of course, starting salaries would be much lower. It is also worth remembering that Washington, DC, a hub for government work at the federal level, has a high cost of living.

FIRST DAYS, YEARS, AND BEYOND

As indicated in the beginning of the chapter, as an individual with an I-O background, you are likely to find yourself working as a human resource generalist, in a specialized department such as training or organization development, or serving as an internal consultant. As is the case with industry, you may be the only person with an I-O background, or one member of a large team of I-O professionals. Different jobs and agencies vary in the potential for development and promotion up the ladder.

From our perspective, one of the exciting but also challenging features of jobs in the public sector is that from day one you are likely to be assigned projects that will have a significant impact on the quality of life of your community, have a high level of visibility, and make a difference. You might be charged with developing a new selection battery for police that will reduce incidents involving excessive force. Your first project could be developing tests that meet the requirements of a consent decree managed by the federal courts. Or, you might be asked to develop an attitude survey to improve the delivery of health care to veterans. If projects like these sound intriguing to you, you should consider going into the public sector.

As indicated earlier, in working for the government as compared to the industrial sector, employees are expected to retain their professional identity and continue to serve as technical experts, even while advancing into managerial and executive levels. Many I-O practitioners may serve in a consultant role, either conducting research or working with government clients.

*****

Those interested in government work may come to have a love-hate relationship with the unique qualities associated with this sector. Compared with the application process in other sectors, the stricter and more drawn out process may be a point of frustration. However, there are opportunities for varied skillsets and specializations, and the context of the work has a direct and powerful impact on a certain community or even the country, which is seen as exciting and rewarding for those in government roles.

PART 5

CONCLUDING THOUGHTS

CHAPTER 15

Concluding Thoughts

If you have made it this far, we want to take a moment to thank you for your kind attention and for your patience. Our main goal in writing this was to work toward making I-O Psychology more accessible, by creating an easy resource for those who might have heard of the field and want to learn more. Whether you are reading this as a high school student considering different possibilities, a college student finishing up a Psychology degree and unsure of your next steps, a working professional considering going back to school, or someone in an entirely different occupation, we hope that you have found this book helpful in giving you a glance into what I-O Psychology is, how to become an I-O Psychologist, and the availability of some of the main career options.

If we are lucky, we may have even convinced a few of our readers to pursue I-O Psychology. For those that are intrigued by this possibility, we would recommend looking beyond our guidance to the vast online resources available. In Table 15.1, we highlight a few starting points for those wanting to begin an exploration of the field of I-O. However, spending just a few minutes online does convince us of the value of a book such as this one on becoming an I-O Psychologist. Unfortunately, the internet is a mix of good advice, bad advice, and just plain, totally wrong advice. If you were somewhat career confused, we hope this book delivered some clarity.

As our field grows and our impact receives more attention in the media, we hope that I-O Psychology continues to increase in public visibility, so that everyone knows it could be a career option. We say this not only so that we can avoid those long explanations when we are asked what we do, which would be nice, but also primarily so that we can continue to grow and improve our field by attracting diverse, talented individuals to be a part of it.

Table 15.1 Online I-O Resources

Careers and Graduate School Applications

SIOP Student Page www.siop.org/studentdefault.aspx	Includes resources on graduate program details and rankings, advice and information related to applications, graduate study, internships, and jobs.
Neoacademic, Richard Landers, Ph.D. neoacademic.com/	Provides detailed resources on preparing for graduate school within an undergraduate timeline as a guide beginning sophomore year.

I-O Content and Research

I/O At Work www.ioatwork.com/	Publishes summaries of published I-O research with a focus on application to the HR world and helping practitioners stay connected to relevant research.
re:work, Google rework.withgoogle.com/	Structured as a collection of research, best practices, and tools for addressing organizational issues within popular I-O areas such as goal setting.
Center for Organizational Excellence, APA www.apaexcellence.org/	Collection of resources such as research articles, abstracts, webcasts, and online courses in working toward increasing public awareness psychology in the workplace.
Workplace Psychology, Steve Nguyen, Ph.D. workplacepsychology.net/	Blog posts focus on I-O related topics with an emphasis on analyzing issues by drawing on research discussed in a clear and digestible manner.

Maybe our bias is showing in saying this, but we think I-O Psychology would be a great career for a lot of different people, interests, and personalities. Whether you are drawn to the classic applications like selection and assessment, or you are intrigued by the quantitative side with coding and crunching the numbers, or you are fascinated by group dynamics and helping teams arrive at the best decisions, or you come from another field that could inform a part of the work we do, we would argue that there is something in it for everyone.

We also want to emphasize once more that there are so many possible career paths and there is no best approach. While we have sometimes relied on assumptions of the more traditional approaches for simplicity (e.g., pursuing graduate school right out of college, or choosing a career in a specific sector), we hope that you have also gathered, through the stories of our contributors, that you can really create your own path in I-O Psychology. We encourage you to try out as many experiences as you need throughout your career to find the optimal fit for you and for your own development.

We know of many successful I-O Psychology professionals who learned of the field through simple serendipity. We could tell you stories of famous, well-known I-O Psychologists who earned Cs as undergraduates, and even as graduate students. Whatever your background, whatever your past life experiences and grades, only you can peer into your heart and determine whether it would be right for you to pursue a degree in I-O Psychology. One of the classic principles of Organizational Psychology is equifinality, which means that a desired end state can be reached in many different ways and through diverse paths. We wish you the best as you follow your own personal journey to career and life fulfillment.

Bibliography

American Psychological Association. (2010). *Publication Manual of the American Psychological Association (6th Ed)*. Washington, DC: APA.

American Psychological Association. (2017). *Ethical principles of psychologists and code of conduct*. Washington, DC: APA.

Cascio, W. F., & Aguinis, H. (2008). Research in industrial and organizational psychology. *Journal of Applied Psychology, 93*, 1062–1081.

Highhouse, S., Doverspike, D., & Guion, R. M. (2016). *Essentials of Personnel Assessment and Selection (2nd Ed)*. New York, NY: Psychology Press.

Levy, P. E. (2017). *Industrial/Organizational Psychology: Understanding the Workplace (5th Ed)*. New York, NY: Worth.

Licensure of Consulting and I-O Psychologists (LCIOP) Joint Task Force. (2017). The licensure issue in Consulting and I-O Psychology: A discussion paper. *Industrial and Organizational Psychology, 10*, 144–181. (Also, all of the replies).

Lowman, R. L. (2006). *The Ethical Practice of Psychology in Organizations (2nd Ed)*. Washington, DC: APA.

Single, P. B. (2009). *Demystifying Dissertation Writing: A Streamlined Process from Choice of Topic to Final Text*. Sterling, VA: Stylus Publishing, LLC.

Strunk, Jr., W., & White, E. B. (2000). *The Elements of Style (4th Ed)*. Boston, MA: Allyn & Bacon.

Zelin, A. I., Lider, M., Doverspike, D., Oliver, J., & Trusty, M. (2014). Competencies and experiences critical for entry-level success for I/O psychologists. *Industrial and Organizational Psychology: Perspectives on Science and Practice, 7*, 70–75.

Zelin, A. I., Oliver, J., Chau, S., Bynum, B., Carter, G., Poteet, M. L., & Doverspike, D. (2015). Identifying the competencies, critical experiences, and career paths of I-O Psychologists: Government. *The Industrial-Organizational Psychologist, 53*(2), 117–126.

Zelin, A. I., Oliver, J., Chau, S., Bynum, B., Carter, G., Poteet, M. L., & Doverspike, D. (2015). Identifying the competencies, critical experiences, and career paths of I-O Psychologists: Industry. *The Industrial-Organizational Psychologist, 53*(1), 142–151.

Zelin, A. I., Oliver, J., Doverspike, D., Chau, S., Bynum, B., & Poteet, M. L. (2015). Identifying the competencies, critical experiences, and career paths of I-O Psychologists: Consulting. *The Industrial-Organizational Psychologist, 52*(4), 122–130.

Zelin, Z. I., Oliver, J., Doverspike, D., Chau, S., Bynum, B., & Poteet, M. L. (2015). Identifying the competencies, critical experiences, and career paths of I-O Psychologists: Academia. *The Industrial-Organizational Psychologist, 52*(3), 149–157.

Zelin, A. I., Doverspike, D., Oliver, J., Kantrowitz, T., & Trusty, M. (2014). Developing career paths for I-O Psychologists: Projects plans and updates. *The Industrial-Organizational Psychologist, 52*(2), 31–46.

Index

Note: Page numbers in **bold** refer to tables. Text boxes are signified by the letters tb and the box number after the page number, e.g. 108tb11.1.